promoting
family
change

promoting family change

The optimism factor

Bronwen Elliott
with Louise Mulroney and Di O'Neil

ALLEN & UNWIN

Allen & Unwin
9 Atchison Street
St Leonards NSW 2065
Australia
Phone: (61 2) 8425 0100
Fax: (61 2) 9906 2218
Email: frontdesk@allen-unwin.com.au
Web: http://www.allen-unwin.com.au

National Library of Australia
Cataloguing-in-Publication entry:

Elliott, Bronwen.
   Promoting family change: the optimism factor.

   Bibliography.
   Includes index.
   ISBN 1 86448 945 6.

   1. Problem families—Australia. 2. Family social work—Australia. 3. Problem families—Australia—Case studies. 4. Family social work—Australia—Case studies. I. Mulroney, Louise. II. O'Neil, Di, 1946– . III. Title.

362.82860994

Set in 11/12 pt Bembo by Midland Typesetters
Printed by SRM Production Services Sdn Bhd, Malaysia

10 9 8 7 6 5 4 3 2 1

Contents

Foreword

Family-centred practice has a long tradition. One of the early writers on working with families was American social work pioneer Mary Richmond, who wrote the following in her book *Social Diagnosis*, published in 1917:

> Family caseworkers welcome the opportunity to see at the very beginning . . . several members of the family in their own home environment, acting and reacting upon one another, each taking a share in the development of the client's story, each revealing in ways other than words social facts of real significance.

Embedded in her words are profound insights that we have come to think of as very modern, such as the notions of individual and family narratives and non-verbal communication. They make modern theories of family change look like old wine in new bottles, which of course is what they fundamentally are, but that is not a bad thing. If successive generations rediscover the same core concepts, albeit expressed in the language of their times, then perhaps this tells us something about enduring truths of family life and how change can occur.

Sometimes a profound idea seems to disappear, almost as if it misses a generation or two. Mary Richmond, along with other family caseworkers of the early part of the twentieth century, was an optimist, but somewhere along the line optimism got lost. Where it went is not so important as the fact that it appears to have returned. Some would say that Freud lost it. Psychoanalytic theory was a powerful double-edged sword, opening up a new way of understanding the inner world but also casting the family in the role of the repressive agent of society. The tradition of pathologising families was continued by the early family therapists. Witness the now discredited notion of the schizophrenogenic family which was thought to be the source of schizophrenia and which deeply damaged many families.

While both psychodynamic and family systems theories have offered valuable insights for those working with families, they have carried within them a way of seeing families that has emphasised the deficits rather than the strengths. This book sets out to redress this. From a perspective of overarching optimism, it introduces the reader to several approaches to working with families that are built on optimism and strengths. Of course, there are risks associated with optimism. As the British child abuse researcher Professor Dingwall has expressed it, the 'rule of optimism' can be very harmful in child protection practice. But the risks associated with pessimism are also great. In the history of child welfare in this country we have inflicted great pain on children and their families through the application of the rule of pessimism.

This book was primarily written for practitioners working outside formal therapy settings with marginalised families who are often demoralised by poverty and violence. Often such families have multiple, immediate needs and they may have been referred by statutory organisations with whom they have had a conflictual history. Such factors are rarely considered in most texts on family work which assume that the family is seeking help voluntarily and that basic material needs in relation to health, housing and income are met. Practitioners will be able to relate to this book, precisely because it does not make such assumptions.

The lessons of the book, however, will also be of value to those working in more formal therapy settings. While focused on four approaches—solution-focused, narrative, cognitive and community-building—its foundation rests not on therapeutic technique but on core principles of family practice. These principles include the old adage of 'starting where the family is', developing respectful relationships, setting goals and helping in practical ways. In clinical contexts, the last is often seen as the 'poor relation' next to the more ix

psychological interventions. This has less to do with what families value than with professional preoccupation with status and upward social mobility. Yet, when we focus on the 'inner world' of the family to the exclusion of the 'outer world', we run the risk of losing sight of the fact that we live our lives in material states of affairs as well as in psychological states of mind. We need to remember to work at the interface of both.

The authors exemplify a 'purposive pluralism': an ability to take theoretical approaches and to see them not as mutually exclusive views of the world, but as overlapping and interrelated lenses through which to understand and respectfully enter the life of a family. Purposive pluralism is not mindless eclecticism, a grab bag of gimmicks that lacks coherence. The authors also affirm the importance of the relationship between the worker and the family. Research suggests that worker qualities such as warmth, genuineness and empathy are more important ingredients that the theory or technique that the worker espouses.

This book heralds an exciting new chapter in the history of family-centred practice. It takes us a long way down the road toward the destination of strength-based family work. Yet it acknowledges what we still don't know: what works with whom and under which circumstances, how to work with families in ways which are more sensitive to cultural differences, and, last but not least, how to work with men more effectively than we have to date. This leaves us a lot of scope for further exploration.

Associate Professor Dorothy Scott
School of Social Work
University of Melbourne

Acknowledgements

This book could not have been written without the contributions of family members and family workers who took time to answer our questions and describe their experiences. Our thanks go to Dave, Debbie, Fiona, Kaz, Kellie, Leonie, Nicole and Stephanie who shared their families' stories of change with us. Only some of their stories have been told in this book, but they all helped to shape our understanding of what change means for families.

During the research for this book, staff from the following family services took part in interviews and linked us with the families who participated. Without their generosity in making time available and their willingness to share their expertise this book could never have been written: Armidale Family Support Service; Barnardo's Children's Family Centre, Auburn; Blacktown Alcohol and Other Drugs Family Support Service; Blue Mountains Family Support Service; Burnside Coffs Harbour Child and Parent Support Service; Burnside Family Work, North Parramatta; Burnside Northern Lakes Family Centre; Centacare Lower North Shore Family Support Service; Dalmar Hills Family Centre; Dalmar Quakers Hill Family Support; Deniliquin Family and Youth Support Services; Granville Family Support; Horizons Central Coast Family Services Inc.; Jannawi Family Centre, Wiley Park; Mercy Family Support Service, Hornsby; Newcastle Family Support Service; Parramatta Holroyd

Family Support; Port Stephens Family Support Service; Riverwood Family Support; St Luke's, Bendigo.

Graham Vimpani, from the University of Newcastle, and Debbie Dagg, from the NSW Department of Community Services, helped us to understand the connections between social capital and community building. Paul Bullen generously provided comments on several drafts of the community building material. Dick Armstrong challenged us to broaden our vision at the beginning of the project and provided valuable feedback towards the end.

The financial assistance of the Ian Potter Foundation made it possible for this book to be written. The support of this Foundation in developing good practice in the field of family work is acknowledged with great thanks.

The Family Support Services Association of NSW has provided financial support for the production of the book and great encouragement to the authors. This reflects the Association's commitment to the promotion of high quality services to families.

Finally, thanks to the many family members, friends and colleagues who helped us to believe that this book was possible!

THE IAN POTTER FOUNDATION

FSSA

Introduction

WHAT IS FAMILY WORK?

Parents start out with hopes and dreams for themselves and their children, yet most parents find that family life is far from simple. For families living in vulnerable circumstances, struggling with issues such as inadequate resources, isolation or disability, it can be all too easy to lose sight of hope and for dreams to fade. Those whose role is to assist families in challenging circumstances can face what seems an overwhelming task. This book has been written as a resource for family workers.

In this book the term 'family work' is used to describe practice that addresses issues affecting the functioning of the family and the relationships between family members. This definition of family work does not assume that all members of the family will be available or willing to be involved. Rather, family work is defined by its focus on family concerns, not by the people involved. While family work will often include active steps to draw family members into the process, family work can be undertaken with one family member, or with many.

While the family is its central concern, family work recognises that all families exist within and are affected by their context. In seeking to enhance the capacities of families to function well, family work attends not only to the internal workings of the family, but also to the family's access to resources and links to the wider community.

WHAT IS THE CONTEXT OF THE FAMILY WORK DISCUSSED IN THIS BOOK?

This book is addressing issues of family work as they confront practitioners outside formal therapy contexts. It is grounded in the reality of work with families who face a range of complex situations, many of which can be linked to socioeconomic disadvantage. Members of these families rarely ring for appointments with a clearly defined issue that they want to address. They often come in contact with a family worker through a circuitous route, which sometimes involves contact with many other agencies. They may have been pressured to accept a family work service, they may be fearful of and reluctant to trust family workers assigned to assist them. Frequently there is little common ground between the family's beliefs about their situation and the views of others around them.

Family work with these families is often conducted under the auspices of community-based organisations or other agencies that operate in a defined local area. Agencies often include a practical component in their service delivery, such as assistance where transport is difficult. The style of practice is informal, often involving work done in the family's home or in other settings, for example, in cars while travelling to appointments. In these contexts it is unusual to gather and engage with all family members for a formal session each time an issue is addressed. The pace of work may be unpredictable, with family workers responding to crises as well as planned sessions.

CURRENT PRACTICE OR THE VERY BEST PRACTICE?

Family work in these less formal contexts has not been well documented. This book opens up this kind of family work and examines how family workers have taken approaches developed outside family work practice and used them in family work settings. Such approaches include those originally developed in more formal therapeutic settings. In particular this book shows how these approaches can serve as a resource for workers when they feel stuck.

Rather than prescribing a preferred model of family work, *Promoting Family Change* deals with the realities and challenges of current practice. Because it reflects current developments in the field, the book can only explore practice to the extent that it exists. For example, the development of family work practices responding to cultural diversity has been largely limited to the employment by some services of indigenous or staff from non-English speaking backgrounds. An Australian statistical overview of family work agencies shows that families from non-English speaking backgrounds are underrepresented among the families accessing those services (Bullen 1998, p. 37). As a result, models for family work paying attention to the challenges of culturally diverse practice have not been developed. There has been little discussion of ways in which family work practice might vary in response to specific culturally determined needs or contexts. Similarly, there are few examples of strategies for providing culturally sensitive family work where the worker and the family have differing cultural backgrounds.

At the same time, this book recognises the need for practice that is respectful and inclusive of families' cultures and specific challenges for family workers in this area are outlined. It is the authors' hope that greater cultural awareness and sensitivity will drive the development of new ideas and strategies, which then can be made available to practitioners.

Similarly the practice described in this book reflects a disproportionate emphasis on the voices of women rather than men. In spite of the steps taken by some services to engage with and involve men more effectively, women remain at present the major consumers of family work services. Moreover, a number of the stories in this book involving men are concerned with men who perpetrate violence within their families. This emphasis is not intended to reinforce stereotypes of men as worthless, or as the major cause of difficulties in families. However, the reality faced by many agencies is that violence within families is often a significant concern to family members, that violence often involves a male partner, and that for workers in the family's home to engage both partners without further jeopardising safety presents many difficulties. While a good case can be made for the need to work with men more effectively, strategies for undertaking such work in a family work setting are only just emerging and are explored in this book.

ARE THE STORIES IN THE BOOK REAL?

This book includes numerous family stories. Brief vignettes drawn from many years of practical experience illustrate different interventions. The names and identifying details are fictitious, and they do not illustrate the circumstances of any individual family.

However, other stories in the text are real. At the end of chapters 3, 4, 5 and 6 family members tell in their own words their experiences of different approaches. Their stories are told with their permission and are very gratefully acknowledged. In addition, many practitioners delivering family work services have been quoted in chapters 7, 8 and 9. Quotes have been acknowledged in the text with the given names and organisational details of the workers concerned.

WHY OPTIMISM?

This book did not begin with a focus on optimism. Originally it aimed to document and describe the way in which particular approaches were being adapted to family work settings. In the past it had been possible to put all family work practice under the broad heading of a 'problem solving' approach. It was becoming apparent that this was no longer appropriate as different approaches were emerging in the field that were distinct from each other. These included solution-focused work, the narrative approach, cognitive therapy and community building.

As the approaches that had been adopted most often by family workers were reviewed, it was clear that there was a common theme between them. Each approach could be described as taking an optimistic stance. In this context optimism is defined as the belief that change is possible, and that the starting point for change is the strengths and capacities of family members.

This position of optimism does not ignore the complex needs of families who live in very vulnerable circumstances. Family workers repeatedly described the ways in which particular approaches outlined in this book assisted them to practise in a way that acknowledged and responded to those circumstances but remained consistent with an optimistic view.

Interestingly, the family members who were interviewed about their experiences of change had many common threads to their stories, regardless of the approach or approaches that had influenced those working with them. Their experiences confirmed that the value of examining different approaches in family work is not because any one approach or combination of approaches offers a recipe for success for families. Rather, the different approaches are a valuable resource to family workers because of the ways in which they encourage a focus on the possibility of change and the family's capacities in the change process.

one

Optimism and family work

'Most days I wonder why I bother to get out of bed. All I can see is mess. I'm a mess, the kids are a mess, the house is a mess. What is the point?' Jen finished her story and looked at Miriam. Miriam shifted in her chair.

Jen, aged 32, was the mother of two children, Lenny aged twelve and Annie aged three. Miriam was a family worker at the local family support service. Jen was referred there when Annie's preschool contacted the statutory child protection service expressing concerns that she was being neglected.

Jen left Annie's father Ron two months ago. Initially Jen had been drawn to Ron's protectiveness but over time, as Ron sought to control the lives of all in the family, Jen and the children were subjected to violence and verbal abuse. Leaving Ron had seemed to be the answer to all the family's problems.

However, as Jen grimly observed, she had jumped out of the frying pan and into the fire. She had substantial credit card debts and was now trying to support the family on welfare payments supplemented by casual bar work. She sometimes needed to leave Lenny and Annie in the house alone at night so she could work. When she worked days she relied on Lenny to wake, dress, feed and deliver Annie to preschool. She felt Lenny had learned a lot of 'bad attitudes' from Ron, his stepfather, and had no respect for her. The family were living in a unit with a leaking roof and Jen had given up trying to keep the flat tidy. 'What's the point,' as she put it, 'when even the landlord doesn't visit?' Piles of washing covered the chairs and the floor, and the lounge room was littered with used crockery.

'Look,' said Jen, 'who could call this a life?'

Miriam could see exactly what Jen meant. Her job is to help Jen and her family find ways to feel more in charge of their lives.

Miriam is one of thousands of family workers who meet families like Jen's each week. These are families struggling with complex situations. They may be dealing, like Jen's family, with issues relating to domestic violence, child protection concerns and poverty. Other families may be affected by the mental illness or disability of a family member, or by substance abuse or addictions. As well as their present difficulties, family members may bring with them the impact of past events such as childhood experiences of disadvantage or abuse.

OPTIMISTIC WORK WITH FAMILIES

Family workers such as Miriam form part of a network of services such as family support services, refuges, neighbourhood centres, family centres and child protection agencies supporting families. Often operating within non-government, community-based organisations, these services have different funding sources, structures and roles. However, a key characteristic found within this diverse range of settings is the optimistic attitude displayed by family workers.

Optimism in this context is not about having a naturally sunny outlook, it is not a statement about workers' personalities, nor is it a generalised hope that everything will be all right eventually. It is an active stance that looks for possibilities for change even when situations appear hopeless. Those who practise optimism in family work believe that change is possible, and that families themselves are capable of bringing about change. The worker's role in this optimistic framework is to mobilise this capacity of the family.

For some workers this optimism is rooted in deeply held values about the capacity of families and individuals. For some it reflects personal experiences of struggle and growth, which have nurtured the belief that others can travel a similar journey. Other workers would talk about challenging labels or self-fulfilling prophecies.

Regardless of the challenges they face and the different backgrounds they come from, optimism abounds among family workers.

Because these workers operate from the same optimistic framework, they share some common ideas about what are helpful ways to assist families facing difficulties.

Starting where the family is

Often family work starts literally where the family is and family workers recognise home visiting as a highly effective strategy. Starting where the family is means listening to the family's story first and finding out what is important to them. Even where the worker's involvement with the family has been triggered by the agenda of some other party, such as a statutory child protection service, the family worker's initial task is to hear the story from the family's point of view. The views of others may have to be taken into consideration in the plans the worker and the family develop, but these views cannot be an effective starting point if the family perspective has not been heard.

Developing respectful relationships

Workers in the helping professions accept the vital importance of respectful relationships in theory. In practice, maintaining respectful relationships can be hard work, especially where clients may have had little experience of being respected themselves. Persisting with respectful behaviour in the face of aggression and hostility, when clients lie or abuse trust or when their actions are damaging to other family members, takes patience.

Family workers may draw on their own life experiences to find encouragement to keep working on respectful relationships. They have their own experiences of struggle with difficult family issues, relationships and parenting. This recognition challenges the 'us and them' view of clients, which can lead to denigrating clients overtly or implicitly, and to limiting workers' beliefs about the potential for change.

Setting goals

Often contact with a family worker is the first time families have been able to tell their story to someone and really feel that they have been heard. Such contact is the base from which family workers can find out what the family's biggest concerns are and help them set some goals for addressing these. Families may be overwhelmed if they have to do too many things at once, so it is important that workers encourage families to start with small steps and negotiate new goals once some of the earlier ones have been achieved. When families are caught up in the chaos of multiple problems, setting goals can encourage a focus on looking for success, not on what is going wrong.

Helping in practical ways

Family workers recognise the value of assistance with practical problems. This could mean finding a way to obtain a cheap washing machine and working out how to get the washing done in the meantime. It may mean going shopping or getting legal advice alongside a parent as a way of teaching skills. Family workers try to find a balance between reducing stress in the family and teaching skills that can help their clients address difficulties independently in the future.

As well as the immediate value of addressing the family's most urgent concerns, working together to solve a practical problem provides an opportunity for the family worker to develop a stronger relationship with the family, and to find out more about family members' concerns and the way they work together.

Building networks

Isolation has a significant impact on families. If parents do not have access to extended family support, if they do not have friends locally, or do not know what services are available, the task of parenting will be much harder. Family workers seek to break down isolation in various ways. Families may be invited to playgroups or coffee mornings, which give them the opportunity to meet other local parents. Services may run groups with a specific focus, such as groups for survivors of domestic violence or parenting groups.

Family workers also provide information about other services that may be relevant to the family and can help the family to gain access to specialised assistance. This may involve addressing practical obstacles such as lack of transport or child care, or other barriers such as suspicion or anxiety.

Building on strengths

Optimistic family work is oriented towards identifying the strengths and resources within families and using them as the base on which new skills and approaches can be developed.

Other approaches to working with families look for change to come from an in-depth exploration of the family's problems and deficits. Such explorations can include looking for the origin of problems, placing problems within categories and using knowledge based on the study of similar problems to expose related problems and predict outcomes.

However, a strengths-based approach doesn't assume a connection between the knowledge about problems and working out what to do about them. In contrast, workers using this approach assume that change is more likely if it can be built on what exists within the family already, rather than being imported from outside.

CHALLENGES TO OPTIMISM

Two months after their first interview, Miriam again climbed the steps to Jen's flat. Miriam knew she had worked hard since their first meeting, but felt dissatisfied with what had been achieved. She had spent a long time talking to Jen, and had heard a lot about Jen's life. She wondered whether hearing Jen's story was helpful as each time they talked Jen seemed to have discovered more to regret.

Miriam tried to set goals with Jen, but each time she visited there seemed to have been a new disaster and Miriam found it hard to maintain a sense of direction. At first it seemed the most important thing was to find alternatives to Lenny and Annie being left at night, since the statutory welfare authorities were concerned about their safety. Then Jen lost her job, so this issue was resolved, but the family faced further financial pressure as a result.

Miriam found it hard to find anything that Jen felt was worth working on. She suggested a group for parents of teenagers and Jen attended the first two sessions, but then decided the problem wasn't Lenny, it was her, so the group couldn't help. Jen didn't want to find out about counselling services, saying, 'What would they know? They couldn't help me.' Miriam suggested a craft group, but Jen wasn't interested in craft. Miriam tried to interest Jen in developing routines for the housework, but Jen felt there was no point when the house was such a mess. Miriam passed on information about Jen's rights as a tenant, but Jen couldn't decide whether to follow this up or simply to move when her lease expired. Miriam wondered why Jen was still keen to see her and found herself half hoping that Jen would forget their appointments or send her away because she hadn't been able to help. She was starting to find that Jen's despair was contagious.

Most, if not all, family workers have had experiences like Miriam's. Like Miriam, they have questioned the value of their work, and wondered whether there were any grounds for optimism about a family like Jen's. In recent years they may have asked these questions more often because of major shifts in the provision of services to children and families.

Several decades ago the frequent response to struggling families was to remove the children from the family and place them in institutional or foster-family care. In the 1970s a range of factors contributed to the development of policies and services aimed at the prevention of placement and the reunification of children who had been removed from their natural family (Scott and O'Neil 1998, p. 24).

For the family support services that began to develop at this time, the initial focus was often on early intervention and prevention of family breakdown. Staff did not necessarily have academic qualifications, but they brought with them the intuitive helping skills they had acquired as family members, carers, and paid or volunteer community workers. The confidence and optimism of staff was fuelled by the success they experienced in their work with families. They used what worked, and it was no great surprise to those who subsequently gained formal qualifications when their tertiary studies confirmed what they already knew were effective practices with families.

However, as the value of family support gained wider recognition, services found their staff were working with families coping with more complex situations. Instead of seeking to prevent family difficulties, staff were working with families who were neglecting or abusing their children, and where there were complex relationship difficulties. Often families were facing major financial and social disadvantages, complicated by other factors such as drug or alcohol use, or mental health issues. Because of their ability to work with families in their homes, and the flexible mix of services they offered, family workers often found themselves working with families that more specialised agencies had difficulty reaching.

In this changing context, family workers found that their ideas about what worked with families often did not take them far enough. They might be able to engage the families who were now being referred to them, to hear their stories, and perhaps to offer some practical help. But support was not necessarily enough for these families. Sometimes workers felt that by supporting the family they were not helping.

At times family workers found they seemed to be putting more work into the change process than the families themselves. Sometimes the more the family worker did to help, the less the family seemed committed to and involved in the work being done. The family worker could be exhausted, but the family situation remained the same. Something needed to change if family members were to stay together and stay safe.

TAKING OPTIMISM FURTHER

Family workers have drawn on the following four approaches to assist them in taking optimism further in their work with families:

* solution-focused
* narrative
* cognitive
* community-building.

A summary of these approaches is provided in chapter 2. They have been chosen because of the place they have in family work in Australia at the present time. Four factors influence this choice.

1   These approaches are widely used in family work agencies. As well as anecdotal evidence of this, the 1998 census of the Family Support Services Association of NSW reported extensive use of narrative, solution-focused and cognitive behavioural therapy by family workers employed in 140 organisations in NSW. The same census reported that 75 per cent of these organisations engaged in community-building activities as part of the family work program (Family Support Services in NSW 1998, pp. 14, 15).

2   The value of these approaches is widely recognised in family and community services. They are well documented, have influenced

family work in a number of countries, and are supported by an extensive practice literature. Reading lists are provided at the end of the chapters detailing each approach.

3 These approaches have been relatively recently adopted by family services. Hence the way in which they have been introduced into organisations within the last decade can be charted and the challenges they have presented can be documented.

4 These approaches are each based on an optimistic framework. Each builds on the same basic assumption that people have the capacity to make change happen, no matter how challenging the situation they may be in. Each of these approaches therefore emphasises the competency of workers to mobilise and build on the resources within families, rather than emphasising specialised knowledge, expertise or insight of workers to create change.

The selection of these approaches should not be taken as evidence that they are proven as the most effective approaches available to family workers. Overall, little research has been undertaken into the effectiveness of these approaches, particularly in the context of family work as opposed to more formal therapeutic settings. The cognitive approach has been extensively evaluated in formal settings, and has been demonstrated to be an effective treatment for depression and other specific difficulties. These studies have not been replicated in a family work setting, and the nature of family work with its attention to the broad range of family issues would make it somewhat difficult to do so.

Although the effectiveness of the community-building approach per se has not been evaluated, it draws on research that has highlighted the influence of social networks on family functioning, and has demonstrated the links between the strengths of a community and the wellbeing of individuals.

At this stage little empirical work has been done to evaluate the solution-focused and narrative approaches. Moreover, these approaches may be difficult to evaluate empirically since they cannot be described in terms of core strategies that a worker would always use.

There are no research findings to indicate whether these four approaches are equally useful, whether different approaches work more effectively with some families rather than others or how these approaches compare with others also available to family workers. This, however, reflects the limitations of empirically-based research in the human services field generally, not just in the area of family work.

Origins of these approaches

We have used the word 'approaches' rather than 'theories' or 'frameworks' deliberately. These approaches can be seen as groupings of ideas about working with families. They have distinguishing features and have been documented in a range of ways. While all have an underlying theoretical base, those theories are drawn from diverse sources, and legitimated in different ways.

The four approaches outlined in this book have not evolved in a vacuum. In a range of ways they draw from decades of theoretical work and practical experience in the human services field. They do not define the limits of family work as it operates in the community sector. Without a doubt the process of evolution and discovery will continue. This will lead to the refinement of these approaches and the development of new ones.

Some of the theoretical ideas underpinning the approaches have been drawn from philosophical and sociological writing. Some have been subjected to scientific research, with control groups and experimental method, while some have evolved from people paying close attention to what has been helpful for families and individuals. This book does not focus on the origins of these ideas, since these are well documented elsewhere. (See the 'Finding out more' sections at the ends of chapters 3–6.)

In some instances the four approaches have developed in more formal or 'clinical' settings, where sessions are conducted in an office on an appointment basis. The fact that these formal services are often described as 'therapy' may raise questions as to whether family workers are now becoming therapists. This idea could worry some people, as family workers may not have the formal educational qualifications traditionally associated with providers of therapy. They also work in settings far removed from the order and quiet of an office counselling room. They could be working with a family in the backyard, sitting in the waiting room of a government office or walking up the aisles of a supermarket.

For the most part, family workers have bypassed any debate about whether they are therapists. They are excited about the way ideas about how change can happen for families can be applied to their work. Their interest doesn't spring from a desire to raise their status, nor from an interest in moving from their current work setting. It comes from their interest in providing quality services to families.

For many families, the notion of therapy is an alien or even frightening one. In rural areas opportunities to access formal therapy services are extremely limited. With ideas that increase their potential as agents for change, family workers can be more effective with families that may never choose, or even have the choice, to access formal therapy.

THE BIGGER PICTURE

While the focus of this book is on specific approaches to family work, it must be emphasised that the context in which these ideas are practised continues to be informed by the overarching understanding of what is helpful in working with families. Far from replacing the core principles outlined at the beginning of this chapter, the increasing use of these specific approaches has assisted workers to discover more about the possibilities of change and the potential of the families and communities.

The four approaches examined in this book are not mutually exclusive, nor are they the only influences on family work practice. There are many other influences on the practice of family workers, including those workers drawing on the approaches described in this book. After decades of research and theorising about families, many ideas about children and families have become embedded in the beliefs and practices of family workers without workers necessarily being aware of the origin of those ideas. Examples of this include understandings of child development, responses to grief and loss, and family life cycle issues.

Workers also share among themselves ideas that have been described as practice wisdom. These ideas about what is helpful for families tend to be based on experience and intuition rather than formal research, and are passed on from worker to worker through observation and discussion.

Family work in the community sector is a particularly fertile place for practice wisdom because of the 'cutting edge' nature of contact with families in crisis. Community-based workers are often the first to see and respond to the impact of issues on families. For example, the first response to domestic violence was at the grass roots, with the establishment of practical strategies for assistance such as women's refuges. Academic interest and research into the issue of domestic violence came much later.

Timely or effective aspects of practice wisdom are likely to become formalised and may stimulate research. This is important because sometimes what has been practice wisdom may later be demonstrated to have no impact or may even be unhelpful in family work.

Broader themes, such as feminism, ideas about inequality and equity, and multiculturalism, also influence the approaches used in family work. These ideas can strongly affect the mission and organisational culture of particular services.

DEVELOPING OPTIMISTIC PRACTICE

The starting point of this book is the practice of family workers, and the differing effects optimistic approaches have had on their work. A range of practices are described, including workers and organisations who have chosen one approach as the predominant influence on their work, and other workers and organisations who consciously choose to be open to a range of influences. This book does not prescribe one or other outcome, but explores the preconditions and implications of these ways of working.

Similarly, while recognising the strong feelings that workers may have about their preferred approach, this book makes no judgements about one approach being superior to another. Such comparisons are of little benefit because of the major differences in the kinds of knowledge reflected in the approaches.

Each of the four approaches discussed in this book is based on explicit assumptions about how change can happen for families and communities. The value of reviewing these approaches is not just in understanding their contribution to practice. There is value in prompting workers to develop a more explicit understanding of their own assumptions about family work and what leads to change. This can equip workers to:

- critically review their own practice
- assess new ideas about work with families in terms of how well they fit with those assumptions, rather than responding primarily because ideas are novel, or are packaged attractively
- use their practice experience to critique theory, rather than feeling forced to fit experience into a particular formula.

OUTSKIRTS OF OPTIMISM

Optimistic approaches are based on the belief that within all families and communities there is the potential for change and that where family workers are alert to this potential the possibilities of change are enhanced. At the same time, the reality of family work demonstrates that a belief in the potential for change does not guarantee that change will happen. Where workers blindly pursue an optimistic view the consequences can be tragic, particularly when vulnerable children are involved. Recognising that optimism is not a panacea, this book examines the implications of the selected approaches on three especially challenging aspects of family work.

Child protection

Situations where children are neglected and abused provide challenges to optimistic practice because of the tension between a belief in the potential of families and the reality of the risks to the child. They are also challenging because of the differing positions taken by professionals working with children and families where abuse and neglect have occurred. Doctors assessing a child's injuries, for example, or statutory workers preparing a case for court are required to catalogue evidence of the family's deficits. This can make it particularly difficult for evidence of the family's strengths to be seen as meaningful.

At the same time, research in child protection has identified a pattern where a range of workers match their expectations of the family to what they believe to be the family's capacity, and view the actions of the parents, in particular, in the most positive light (Reder et al., 1993). The influence of this 'rule of optimism' may lead workers to accept a family's plans for change as if that change had already occurred, or to see one piece of positive information as an indication that all is well. In such circumstances misplaced optimism can lead to negative information about the family being discounted or overlooked. This can result in ongoing harm to children, or even their death. The tension between ensuring the safety of children and encouraging positive change in families is recognised as each approach is reviewed in this book. Consideration has therefore been given to the implications for practice where there are concerns about the safety or wellbeing of children.

Domestic violence

The development of family work over the last two decades has occurred in parallel with the recognition of the prevalence of domestic violence in the community. As part of the frontline response to domestic violence, family workers are primarily concerned about the safety of women and children who are affected by violence. A belief in the potential for change can be sorely tested when family workers are confronted with family members unable to leave violent situations, or where women are pursued by a violent partner after they have left the relationship. Challenges to an optimistic stance can arise when considering the potential for change in domestic violence situations, particularly when examining strategies for working with perpetrators of violence.

Poverty

While the effect of poverty on families is widely recognised as a social policy issue, family workers confront the day-to-day impact of poverty on individual families and communities. Family workers have the opportunity to challenge stereotypes of people living in poverty, but also must recognise that no amount of 'positive' thinking in itself can change the macroeconomic and social environment in which individual families live. At the same time, where families see themselves primarily as victims, they may be discouraged from taking any positive action and experience further disadvantage as a result. The challenge is to find the most hopeful points at which small positive changes could begin. Ways in which these approaches can assist in this process are identified throughout this book.

CHALLENGE OF CHANGE

Change invariably brings challenges. Family workers will find it challenging to take on board new ideas about their work, particularly when such ideas may have originated in a different kind of setting. Family workers who have felt comfortable with the approach they have developed over years of experience may question whether a new approach will be compatible with their intuitively developed 'practice wisdom'. Similarly, colleagues from more formal therapeutic settings may find it challenging to hear family workers speaking a similar language, or defining what they do in more theoretical terms. For professionals whose vision of community-based family support services has focused primarily on the practical nature of their work, it may be unsettling or even threatening to perceive that new dimensions are being added. Such responses challenge family workers to ensure that new directions they pursue benefit families.

As she thought about her contact with Jen, Miriam couldn't help comparing her situation to other families where she felt her involvement really did make a difference. She remembered other parents who told her their life stories, sharing with her personal details they had never told anyone before. She remembered other families who had lots to cope with but who found using Miriam as a sounding board helped them work out where to start. Why had her involvement helped those families to make changes, but did not seem to be helping Jen?

Looking at this situation forced Miriam to think hard about why she worked with families in the way she did. What was her role in kick-starting the process of change? As she thought about it, Miriam recognised that for some families just talking about their story to someone who had time to listen, and who was accepting rather than judgemental, was enough for them to see their situation in a new light. They felt better about themselves and were able to start thinking up their own ideas about what to do next, using Miriam as a resource. But with Jen the more they talked, the more stuck things seemed. Miriam started thinking about how she could do something different . . .

two

Four optimistic approaches to family work

When a family worker like Miriam looks for ways to work differently with families, there are a range of approaches she could utilise. Each of these approaches lends a different flavour to the work with Jen and her family. This chapter will provide an overview to four approaches to family work:

- solution-focused
- narrative
- cognitive
- community-building.

While these approaches share an optimistic view of the potential of families and communities to change, they represent the ways different kinds of knowledge inform and challenge workers' assumptions and give new ideas for practice.

SOLUTION-FOCUSED WORK WITH FAMILIES

As its name implies, solution-focused work is concerned with discovering what works. Interest is focused on what people are doing when the problem is absent, or less of a problem, rather than on working out what has gone wrong. Fundamental to this approach is the understanding that knowing more about the problem does not lead to knowing more about answers.

A person experiencing difficulties is likely to find that problems attract lots of attention. They start to dominate encounters with friends, family members and agencies. As conversations become more problem-saturated, the person starts to be identified as the problem, and their ability to see solutions is inhibited. In fact, because of their status as 'the problem', any ideas they generate are likely to be over-looked or dismissed by those around them.

Often other people offer or even force solutions to the situation on the person. In this situation the person with the problem may view themselves as unable to cope and dependent on the answers of others. Alternatively they may reject the advice, find themselves without support and are labelled as resistant. Solution-focused work identifies problem-saturated approaches as leading to discouragement and dependence.

Solution-focused work recognises that the impact of would-be problem solvers can be destructive to the family's capacity to find solutions, and instead emphasises the importance of the family in directing the work they undertake. While many workers express the desire to empower families, within the solution-focused approach the worker's role is not to give power to the family but to stand aside as the family take control of the change process as much as possible. Within this approach the family define the issues and decide the goals of intervention. The family's strengths and solution-finding ability are the focus.

Family-directed practice does not mean workers have nothing to do. In fact it can be a hard task for a worker to sit back, listening carefully to the family, resisting the temptation to jump in with solutions or to get ahead of the family. While the family will generally set the goals of intervention, the worker may play a role in identifying issues and assisting the family in the process of setting goals that are explicit and manageable.

The worker has a key role to look confidently for exceptions to the problem. Their ability to find out more about 'exceptional' behaviour will provide vital clues for the family to explore. Concentrating on what the family already does well nurtures confidence and hope, and provides a framework on which the family can build. Where agency and community resources are available to complement the family's resources, the worker can assist the family to access these.

Solution-focused work is directed toward change, and the identification and measurement of change by the family are vital.

Noticing change enhances optimism about the possibility of further change and finding out what is working gives the basis for setting future goals and identifying solutions. Ongoing evaluation is not confined to the family's experience. The family are seen as expert not only in evaluating their own performance, but in assessing the effectiveness of workers.

Solution-focused practitioners have developed a range of techniques and materials for assisting families to identify strengths and resources, look for exceptions to the problem and measure change. These can be exciting and fun for families and workers to use, and some of them will be discussed in chapter 3. But the core of the solution-focused approach is not in its techniques or its vocabulary but in its fundamental assumptions. Talking about strengths will not make any difference if workers are unable to put aside a preoccupation with the family's problems, if they confuse worker identification of strengths with the family's recognition of them or if they are unable to trust the family to implement their own solutions. Workers must believe that families have the capacity to find solutions.

Solution-focused work and Jen's family

Working within a solution-focused approach, Miriam decided she would focus on:

- what is working for Jen
- assisting Jen to set explicit and manageable goals so she experiences more problem-free occasions
- helping Jen and her family to notice and measure change.

Miriam paid close attention as Jen told her story, and acknowledged the pain and frustration that Jen had experienced. At the same time Miriam listened for anything that could be seen as an exception to the problems Jen felt overwhelming her.

For example, when Jen commented that she wondered why she bothered to get out of bed given the mess she faced, Miriam agreed that it would be understandable if she did stay in bed all day, and gently asked how Jen managed to find the strength to get up when she felt like that. Jen commented that she couldn't stay in bed because the children needed her, and Miriam affirmed her commitment to her responsibilities as a parent.

When Jen expressed the view that leaving Ron had just created new difficulties, Miriam acknowledged Jen's frustration that, after taking such a big step to try and improve her situation, she found herself with new challenges to face. But she also highlighted Jen's recognition of the right of her children and herself to live in a household without violence, and noted that she hadn't given up and returned to a violent household even when tempted to do so.

Miriam was careful to convey the fact that she understood that life for Jen was tough. She didn't try to talk Jen into believing that things weren't that bad. But as she noticed more examples of Jen's competence even in the face of adversity, she found that Jen started to look more relaxed and talked with more animation. Over a couple of sessions Miriam involved Jen, Lenny and Annie in a process of identifying the strengths of the family and family members, and working out what they wanted to be different. They looked at what had worked, and what they could learn from that.

From those conversations a lot of information emerged about things that family members could do. In spite of the chaos at home, Jen cooked a meal each night for the family. Jen was resisting the temptation to go back to Ron, who she saw when he had occasional contact with Annie. Jen had found that the next couple of days after she saw Ron were tough, and she found it helped to make sure she did something on those days that she hadn't been able to do with Ron, such as watching a quiz show on television. Jen started to fill in Miriam on more ideas she had about resisting the temptation to go back to Ron.

Lenny was good at athletics and had competed for his school. He knew about practising new skills as he had recently been learning a new way of high jumping. He wasn't happy about Jen working, but he had been reliable in getting Annie to preschool. And although he acknowledged that he and Jen had had lots of arguments lately, these hadn't carried over into 'attitude' problems at school. Annie could dress herself, and was a good friend to other children at preschool.

Recognising their achievements in the face of adverse circumstances helped Jen and her children to feel a bit more confident that things could change. Miriam remembered what Jen had said at their first visit—'Who could call this a life?'—and explored with her what a life for the family would look like.

This discussion helped Jen to work out the goals for change that meant the most to her. Miriam also included Lenny and Annie in the process of figuring out where the family could start in their effort to 'get a life'. She acknowledged the family's desire to live without feeling that the statutory child protection department needed to check up on them, and asked them to consider life with nothing to justify this intrusion.

When it seemed as though the list of things they needed to do to get the Department out of their lives was overwhelming, Miriam drew on Lenny's experience from athletics training to find out about helpful ways to put new skills into practice. They figured out that it was important not to try to work on too many areas at once, not to push themselves too hard early on and to practise as often as they could.

The first goal the family set was to find a way of making sure Lenny and Annie's safety wasn't compromised by Jen's work. This was urgent because the child protection department had indicated that it wasn't acceptable for Jen to rely on Lenny. While Jen felt she had made the best arrangement she could with the resources she had, she recognised that she would have to make a different arrangement if she wanted the child protection department to leave her alone. She also felt that she had probably been expecting too much of Lenny. As she put it, she'd got him running a marathon when he'd only been in training for the sprints. Jen wanted to keep her job because she needed the money, but decided she couldn't find a way of working at night and making sure the kids were safe. She started looking for day work, which didn't pay as well, but meant she didn't need to rely on Lenny so much.

Jen felt that if she could do a big clean-up it would be easier to keep the flat tidy. Miriam agreed to help her and they spent two days sorting the flat out. They worked out where most of the mess accumulated and Jen thought of some ways of getting in first to avoid it, for example, putting clothes away and ironing them later. As Jen put these plans into practice, she and Miriam monitored the situation to see which plans worked and which didn't. Jen set up a fairly complicated jobs chart for the children on her own. Miriam thought it might be too much for Lenny and Annie to handle, but she waited for the family to try it out. In the end Jen decided it was an Olympic-level chart when what they really needed was Little Athletics, and she set up a new chart with Lenny and Annie.

Miriam put Jen in touch with a tenants' advice service who gave her information about her rights and the owner's responsibilities regarding repairs. When the owner made only minimal repairs to the property, the advice service suggested that Jen could take further action through a tribunal. Jen considered this, but felt that it would be a big hassle and could make it harder to get rental accommodation in future. She decided to wait until her lease ran out in two months' time and then look for somewhere else to live. This would give her some time to look around. She also used the tribunal's information to put some pressure on the agency that managed the property to give her a reference, which would give her a better chance when she found a new flat.

Although Miriam felt that the owner of Jen's flat deserved to be taken to the tribunal, she recognised that Jen's strategy would achieve her goal of improving the family's accommodation and that Jen had to make her own decision about how much stress she could handle.

Six months after Miriam's first contact with the family, they were settled into a new flat, which was smaller but in much better condition than their old one. Jen had found part-time work in a sandwich shop and with the help of a financial counselling service had renegotiated her debts. Lenny was more cheerful and was continuing his interest in athletics. Jen and Lenny were working at getting on without fighting. Since lots of their arguments were about Lenny's responsibilities at home, the jobs chart had helped make sure they were both clear about what he had to do. Annie also had a job to do each day. Lenny said that she would need a lot of coaching to get up to speed, but at least she was in training.

Jen said she still had her 'down' days, but that it had been a while since she even considered going back to Ron. She said the family had gone from having no life to having achieved $\frac{7}{10}$ of a life, and they were going well.

NARRATIVE WORK WITH FAMILIES

A narrative is a story. Listening to the family's story is something every family worker does. When family members tell their story, they cannot possibly mention everything that has happened to them. Some things are highlighted, while others are left out altogether. The stories people tell are edited depending on how they make sense of experiences. When someone tells a story they don't just describe events, but communicate the meaning they have given to them.

Explanations of events or experiences that are endorsed within a particular culture or community have a powerful influence over the way people make sense of things. These endorsements can come via the media, or from individuals or groups who have status in the family's life, such as particular professionals or significant family members.

Narrative work suggests that there are many 'dominant' stories about the experiences of families that are associated with blame and labelling. Guilt, fault, blame and other versions of failure or inadequacy are common themes in these problem-saturated stories. These 'problem stories' don't just affect the way family members tell their stories, but can also lead to people taking on or internalising an identity dominated by the influence of the problem.

For example, a mother may experience her child's behaviour as challenging. Her view of her role as a parent may be influenced by ideas from those around her, such as 'bad children have bad parents', 'your job is to love your child unconditionally' and 'you have to show him that you're boss'. If her own childhood was unhappy, she may be especially vulnerable to suggestions that, because she has been 'damaged', she will be incapable of really loving her child. Under the influence of these ideas, her account of herself as a parent may well reflect ideas of guilt, inadequacy and self-blame.

Problem stories are also associated with prescriptions about what people need to do in the face of problematic experiences. If these prescriptions fail to 'work', families can feel even more powerless.

Narrative work has evolved from the application of ideas about knowledge and meaning that are sometimes described as 'postmodern'. 'Deconstruction' is a term used in postmodern thinking for the process of analysing the way that particular understandings or readings of events and experiences are developed. Narrative work sees deconstruction as inviting the opportunity for reconstruction as people develop preferred alternative accounts of their experiences and identity.

Narrative work involves family workers putting aside the view that they know what is best for people. In asking questions they are not trying to steer the family towards a particular discovery; they are trying to open up possibilities and experiences. This stance is sometimes described as 'not knowing'.

Since narrative work assumes that there are endless possible stories, it does not aim to uncover the 'right' story, but to open up space for an examination of stories. This allows new possibilities for family members to emerge, possibilities that previously have been suppressed by the operation of the dominant story. The expression 'therapeutic conversation' is sometimes used to describe the flavour of this process.

By finding ways to talk about the problem as 'out there' rather than internal to the person, new possibilities for change can be explored. This process is often described as 'externalising' the problem. As the problem is externalised there is room for discussion about its influence in the life of the family. Particular attention is paid to 'unique outcomes' or 'sparkling events' where family members have had an experience that stands out from the problem-dominated story. The meaning of these events is explored through questioning. The worker is not trying to convince the family of the events' meaning, but initiates a process that encourages the family to notice alternative meanings.

In particular, this approach encourages families that have struggled under the influence of blame, guilt and self-doubt to develop pre-ferred stories, highlighting examples of survival, self-care and protest. This can be seen not just as rewriting the family's story, but as the emergence of a new identity for family members.

Central to this process is the development of more and more threads to the emerging story since the 'thicker' the new story, the better able it will be to persist and grow. The most immediate source of threads will be the revisiting of past experiences and the discussion of the family's present experiences in the light of the emerging story. Other ways of creating richer stories are discussed further in chapter 4.

The family may be encouraged to look for other audiences for their story. Who else may be a witness to aspects of their lives that have been overlooked? This process may involve thinking of signifi-cant people in the family's past and reflecting on what they saw or might see now, which can add to the story. It may involve inviting people from the family's past or present to be involved in the process, or looking beyond the family to find someone else who has qualities that equip them for this role. This audience might include other people whose own stories of survival can assist the family in identi-fying knowledge that could be useful.

Because narrative work involves ideas about working with families that may feel very different from those family workers are used to, it can be tempting to see this work primarily in terms of techniques, such as externalising the problem. But, to family workers using narrative ideas, strategies are secondary. Central to narrative work is respect for the family and a belief that once space can be made for new stories, new possibilities can emerge.

Narrative work and Jen's family

Using a narrative approach, Miriam decided her work would focus on the development of a new story for Jen and her family. This story would enable the family to explore new possibilities for change in their circumstances. Miriam will do this by:

- looking for unique outcomes that may point to an alternative story
- making the emerging story 'thicker'
- encouraging Jen to look for an audience to support the new story.

While Miriam listened to Jen's story, she paid close attention to the language Jen used when she talked about her family's experiences. When Jen said, 'Who could call this a life?' Miriam made a mental note. She began tentatively to ask some questions about the ways in which Jen, in spite of all the pressures, had managed to enhance life for herself and her children. Whereas Jen's depiction of her decision to leave Ron had been emphasising the new difficulties that had arisen since she had left, Miriam asked her questions about how she had managed such an enormous step to act for life in the face of many obstacles.

Miriam found out that Jen had planned to leave several times but for different reasons had not. One time Ron had discovered that she had been saving money to help with the move, and had taken it. Another time she had been about to leave when the children got sick, and the momentum had been lost. Finally, one evening Ron had hit her and when Annie got out of bed to find out what was happening she was almost hit by a chair that Ron had thrown. The knowledge that even Annie was at risk from Ron's violence horrified Jen, who had previously believed that she and Lenny were at least partly to blame for setting off Ron with their 'bad tempers'. That time she had decided she had to go.

As Jen recounted these events, Miriam began to explore what they might mean to her. When Miriam asked, 'What does it say about you that you could take this step?' Jen started to cry and said, 'It says that I love my children very much'. Jen then talked about her fear that she wouldn't be able to manage on her own. 'I'm no good at coping on my own,' she said.

Miriam left Jen with some questions to think about, including: 'Who else would be aware of the strength of your ability to love? What have they seen that would have alerted them to this?' She also discussed with Jen the importance that family members were safe. Because of the actions Jen had already taken, Miriam recognised these were concerns Jen shared. This led into a discussion of the concerns the child protection service had about the safety of Jen's children while she was working. Jen decided to ask a girlfriend to come and stay over the next evening when she was working, which gave her some time to think about how best to handle the situation in the future.

A week later Miriam arrived at Jen's flat with a sense of anticipation. However, she was greeted at the door by Jen still in her dressing gown and clearly distressed. She had had to leave work early to pick up the children and as a result had been sacked. To make matters worse, Jen had just received a disconnection notice from the electricity service and since she would have no work in the next week, she had no way of paying the overdue bill. Her most urgent concerns were that the power would be cut off and the child protection service would remove the children.

Miriam knew there were ways to address the problem with the electricity service. At the same time she was conscious of the doubts that Jen had raised the previous week about her ability to cope on her own. By talking over the situation she might reinforce Jen's picture of herself as unable to cope. She checked out what ideas Jen had about dealing with the situation. Jen had noticed a telephone number on the bill to ring if there were problems with payments but said she didn't know what to say. Together they worked out what information Jen would need to provide, then Jen went down to a public telephone and made the call. She was given the name of an organisation that might be able to assist her. Miriam offered to give her a lift there and Jen was able to obtain some assistance to keep the power on.

Miriam was uncertain what to expect the next time she saw Jen. She wondered if Jen could even recall anything of their discussion at their first meeting, given the pressure of day-to-day events. She decided to find out whether Jen recalled the questions Miriam had asked her to think about, and then work out what to do next. To Miriam's surprise Jen had remembered 'that you asked me who else knows that I am a loving person'. Jen began to talk about her grandmother who, she said, 'taught me to love' in spite of a difficult family situation where Jen often felt unloved. 'You know how we were talking before about acting for life?' Jen said. 'Well, love is on the side of life.'

After these comments a conversation developed about the experiences Jen knew to be on the side of life, and those that were associated with taking away from life. Through this conversation Jen and Miriam explored the way in which Jen had experienced violence, blame, guilt and fear as taking away from life. Miriam asked Jen about how she had maintained her capacity to stand on the side of life in spite of Ron's violence and her earlier growing-up experiences. Jen talked about how for a while she had felt that the violence was her fault, and Ron would emphasise this by talking about how frustrating she was to live with. Now she sometimes could believe that it was not her fault, but when she and Lenny argued she started to worry again about whether there was some-thing wrong with her. Miriam asked some questions about the times when Jen was able to stand up to self-blame, which led into a discussion of what else, besides love, was on the side of life. Miriam asked Jen how she thought their conversation was going. Jen said, 'I thought you would tell me what to do, so it feels a bit funny that you mainly ask questions! I'm not sure sometimes how it's going to help, but today I feel more like I'm on the side of life and that feels good.'

Miriam then asked some questions about what Annie and Lenny might be noticing about their mother's standing more strongly on the side of life. Jen talked about the way she had coped with Annie's visit with Ron the previous weekend, and the way she had been able to share Annie's excitement over the movie they had seen, in spite of Jen's feelings of resentment that it was Ron who got to have 'fun time' while she was left with the hard work. She also reflected on the pressure Lenny must have felt since they had left Ron. Miriam wondered aloud about whether Annie and Lenny were bystanders, barrackers or team players in the quest to be more strongly on the side of life.

The next time Miriam visited Jen, Lenny and Annie were at home. Jen had kept them at home and she initially asked Miriam to 'talk some sense to them'. It became apparent that Jen had had a tough week. Annie had told her that 'Dad would let me stay up' when Jen asked her to go to bed. Lenny had been surly and had come home late the previous night. Miriam discovered that Annie and Lenny had noticed some changes in their mum, but were a bit confused by them. They thought she was happier, but also that she was 'on their backs more'. A conversation developed about the project Jen was undertaking to stand on the side of life. Lenny knew a bit about projects because he had done them at school, both on his own and in a team. Miriam discussed what it might be like to be on Jen's project team. Miriam asked Jen and the children what kind of 'good sense' they could contribute.

Over the next couple of months some other people were invited to join Jen's team for life. They included one of Lenny's teachers, who helped him find some 'good sense' when he had some difficulties with peers at school. Jen's grandmother was a founding member, and Jen hung her photo in her bedroom as a reminder. Jen renewed contact with an old friend who had dropped out of Jen's life because she didn't like how Ron treated the family. This friend was thrilled to have the opportunity to be included in Jen's life again. She had also left a violent relationship and was able to recognise Jen's achievements in regaining life. Jen found it helpful to ring her when times were tough.

Jen was able to find a part-time job during the day and, although money was tight, she was able to manage. She decided not to take the neglectful owner of the flat she rented to the tenants' tribunal, but was able to find better accommodation, which she saw as a really important step. She still had arguments with Lenny, and her doubts about her ability to be a good parent were the ones most likely to push her away from the side of life. But she felt her project had been so successful that she was on the side of life for good.

COGNITIVE WORK WITH FAMILIES

Over the last twenty years there have been major developments in the treatment of individuals affected by depression and anxiety. Previously such issues were commonly seen as symptoms of underlying disorders. For example, depression was sometimes seen as an indication that an individual was repressing feelings of anger. To affect change the underlying problems needed to be unearthed and addressed. Within cognitive approaches, however, the feelings of depression or anxiety themselves were seen as the problem. The source of these feelings was explained as habits of thinking. Feelings could be changed if ways of thinking changed. Since actions also influence thoughts and feelings, intervention can include strategies that address what an individual does as well as how they think.

Cognitive approaches were initially developed by psychologists or psychiatrists working in clinical settings. Their work was carefully researched and documented in handbooks. This allowed other clinicians to duplicate the key features of their work. However, the influence of these ideas has extended far beyond formal treatment sessions and beyond work with depression and anxiety to issues such as drug and alcohol abuse.

People affected by depression, anxiety and other issues related to habits of thinking do not necessarily see how they think or feel as their most urgent concern. They might look for help managing their children, they might be admitted to a refuge or they might seek help with budgeting. They might be reported to a child protection service because their children have been neglected or they might ask a family service for help because they cannot cope at home.

Family workers have found it helpful to use cognitive approaches in their work with families because patterns of thinking can influence the capacity of family members to learn new skills and consider different ways of looking at their situation. Recognising the disabling effects of depression and anxiety, family workers may recommend further assessment by a psychiatrist or a psychologist, and they may then work cooperatively with the psychiatrist or psychologist and the family to address the family's concerns.

Cognitive work assists individuals to identify thoughts and note their connections with feelings. Once thoughts are identified, the beliefs reflected in those thoughts can be tested. Challenging those beliefs, because they are illogical, they do not fit with the facts or they do not help, can lead to the development of different beliefs and alternative habits of thinking. As information about the individual's experiences emerges, a picture may develop of the factors that supported the development of particular ways of thinking. For example, abusive treatment as a child or a major loss may be powerful influences on a person's beliefs. The family worker can use this picture of the way the individual's beliefs developed to structure the way they intervene. Practising within the family work framework described in chapter 1, family workers would continue to emphasise family strengths and goals in a respectful way, while also asking questions about a family member's patterns of thinking.

Questioning is an important part of cognitive behavioural work. As well as asking questions to develop a picture of the individual's thoughts and feelings, questions are used to encourage individuals to become aware of this information for themselves. In addition to open-ended questioning, some set techniques have been developed to assist in the testing of beliefs. Education is also important. Information about the relationship between thoughts and feelings, and strategies for encouraging more rational thoughts, is made available.

The value of homework tasks is emphasised; for example, keeping records can highlight the connections between thoughts and feelings and unproductive ways of thinking. Tasks may also focus on achieving behaviour change through strategies such as following a timetable of activities or practising a new skill that has been rehearsed during a session.

Cognitive approaches encourage workers to maintain their focus on clearly defined and achievable goals in the context of a collaborative relationship. These approaches challenge the view that the impact of the past is permanent.

Cognitive work and Jen's family

Using a cognitive approach, Miriam decided that her work would focus on assisting Jen to:

- evaluate her beliefs
- develop new ways of thinking that would help Jen bring changes into the life of her family.

When Miriam met Jen she was struck by Jen's conviction that everything was her fault. In a short period of time Jen blamed herself for having left Ron, for placing the family in debt, for having met Ron in the first place and not realising what he was really like, for not being able to rent a decent flat, for not being able to cope with the house and for not being a good mother for her children. Miriam wasn't surprised that Jen felt trapped and hopeless. She also recognised that Jen had very low expectations about what they might be able to achieve in their time together. Jen felt she had to cooperate to appease the child protection service, but she really couldn't see much point in Miriam spending time with her. Miriam persisted in spite of this, listening carefully and sensitively asking Jen about the family's experiences.

Recognising the negative pattern of Jen's thinking, Miriam decided to start with something small and practical. As she talked with Jen it was evident that Jen was frustrated by her inability to cope with the housework. She said that, while she had never been especially house-proud, in the past she had never been as ashamed of where she lived as she was now. Miriam asked Jen if she would be willing to undertake a small experiment. She suggested that Jen keep a record of any time she spent doing housework. Her record should note what she did and how she felt while she was doing it. Miriam suggested that that information might help Jen to start planning a schedule of housekeeping activities. Cautiously Jen agreed to keep the record.

Miriam and Jen also discussed Jen's concern about the expectations of the child protection service. Miriam focused on Jen's fear that the service would remove the children and asked some questions about this. Jen recognised that the major concern of the child protection service was with the children's supervision. Although Jen had many concerns about her competence as a parent, a number of these were not shared by the child protection service. Miriam suggested that Jen look at the arguments for and against working at nights, since this was the reason for difficulties about the children's supervision. She and Miriam worked out a short-term solution for the next time Jen had to work by Jen's asking a girlfriend to come and stay overnight. This would give her time to look for a longer term solution.

The next time Miriam met with Jen she asked about the housekeeping schedule. Jen had kept a record for a few days and then had lost it. Her main worry now was her financial situation and her concern about how to keep earning enough money while making sure the children were adequately supervised. Miriam responded positively to the effort Jen had made to keep the schedule for even part of the time, especially given her other concerns. Miriam asked Jen whether she thought the schedule was a fair indication of her housekeeping activity. Jen commented that to her surprise she had actually done more housework during the time she had been keeping the record. In fact, she had been reminded of some of the things she had done in the past to keep on top of the housework, and had put one or two of these into practice. For example, she had decided to hang the washing on the clothesline first thing in the morning. Miriam then asked Jen how she had felt when she put these ideas into practice. Jen said, 'I don't feel anything, really.'

Jen agreed to have another go, this time setting a schedule for how and when some of the housework would be done. She decided to hang the washing out first thing each morning, to make sure the dishes were done before going to bed at night and to put away the washing when she brought it in rather than leaving it in piles around the house. To help her get started, Miriam helped Jen to clean up the clothes that were lying around waiting to be put away.

Jen had decided that she needed to give up night work, but she was concerned about how she would manage financially. She was worried about her debts and felt pressured to pay them off. Miriam discovered that Jen hadn't discussed her situation with her creditors. She suggested Jen see a financial counsellor so she would be able to negotiate a repayment scheme with her creditors. In that way she could make the situation more manageable. Miriam rehearsed with Jen what she might say to the counsellor and arranged an appointment.

On her next visit Miriam noticed an immediate difference in the condition of the flat. Jen had stuck to her schedule and had added some responsibilities for Annie and Lenny. While the flat was tidier, however, Miriam noted that Jen continued to be down on herself. In fact she hadn't attended the appointment with the financial counsellor because she had decided there wasn't any point.

Miriam decided to highlight some beliefs Jen had about her life. Miriam had gathered from Jen that her childhood had been unhappy. Her father drank heavily and had been violent. Jen and her sister learned that it made life easier for their mother if they were compliant and kept out of their father's way. Miriam commented on how Jen's early history had encouraged her to believe that if anything went wrong it was her fault. She noted that Jen worked hard at making things right. With Ron, Jen had tried to do everything the way Ron wanted so that their relationship would be a success. If anything went wrong, regardless of whether it was Jen's responsibility or not, she was likely to feel she was to blame. As she had increasingly felt that she was at fault, she had become less and less confident in her ability to do anything right.

Jen commented that she had been thinking of going back to Ron because she couldn't manage on her own. Together Jen and Miriam considered the arguments for and against returning to Ron. They talked about whether just because Jen felt she was to blame, she was really at fault. Jen remembered that sometimes she had been blamed for things that weren't her responsibility.

In the following weeks Jen and Miriam had several more discussions about the pros and cons of Jen's relationship with Ron. Jen ultimately decided that even though aspects of life were easier with Ron, she did not want to live with someone who made her feel guilty and at fault so much of the time. Jen started to be able to identify times when she felt better about herself and life. She was able to resume some contact with friends that had ceased during her relationship with Ron. She started to feel more capable with the housework and although the poor condition of the flat annoyed her, she didn't see it as her fault that the roof leaked.

Jen's growing confidence was challenged when she discovered Lenny was in trouble at school, truanting and getting into fights. She told Miriam later how her initial response was to blame herself, seeing Lenny's behaviour as her fault, because of Ron. Initially she covered up for Lenny and then she tried to talk the school into excusing his behaviour altogether. Later, however, she decided that, regardless of the family's experiences, at some point Lenny and Annie were going to have to learn to be responsible for what they did. She was able to find a teacher who understood that while, on the one hand, Lenny had had a tough time, on the other, with support he could get his act together. Lenny overcame the difficulties and Jen felt she had managed the situation differently from how she might have previously.

Several months after the appointment she missed Jen went to see the financial counsellor and was able to negotiate a more manageable payment scheme for her debts. She was particularly pleased when she was able to locate a new flat, which was in good condition. She felt that she had learned some new strategies for dealing with problems, that she was less likely to believe that everything was her fault and that she was able to 'give herself a pep talk' when she felt things getting on top of her. She recognised that she wasn't a perfect parent, but she felt she was learning to manage situations with Lenny and Annie better than before, and she didn't panic as much when she made mistakes. She still had 'down' days, but they were much less likely to stop her from getting on with life.

COMMUNITY BUILDING

What do families need to have a good quality of life? A roof over their heads, opportunities for employment and adequate income would be a start. But not everything that is needed for a good quality of life has a monetary value attached to it. It is hard to put a price tag on the experience of getting to know a range of people in your neighbourhood, feeling that you can influence decisions that affect you and seeing your children growing up with an expectation that people outside the family circle can be trustworthy.

The idea of social capital has been developed as a way of highlighting the importance of some of these experiences, which are outside the financial structures of our society, but are essential for a good quality of life. If, as Australian writer Eva Cox (1995) puts it, 'we are social beings rather than economic beings' (p. 2), we cannot afford to ignore the importance of our connections with other people. Cox sees social capital as an indicator of the quality of the relationships we have with other people and describes it as referring to 'the processes between people which establish networks, norms and social trust and facilitate coordination and cooperation for mutual benefit' (p. 15). To put it another way, social capital is like a web linking and connecting people, constantly being rewoven as a product of people's interactions.

The community-building approach focuses on creating this web and encouraging relationships that contribute to social capital. These kinds of relationships are likely to feature:

- *Contact with people outside familiar boundaries:* Cox emphasises that social capital is not the same as social cohesion. A community that excludes newcomers or encourages cliques will experience limits on its capacity to create social capital.
- *Trust:* Social capital is dependent on the ability of individuals to work together, putting aside their immediate interests because of a shared concern. As this process is repeated over the life of a shared project, trust grows.
- *Reciprocity:* 'What goes around comes around.' Social capital is developed in situations where individuals perform acts without a specified reward. This is very different from actions that are part of the creation of financial capital, where work and payment go together. However, even when the motivation for a particular act is altruistic, individuals expect that if people help each other generally, when they personally need help, others will provide it.
- *A contribution to the common good:* It is not hard to think of organisations such as street gangs or religious sects in which reliance on the group is essential and loyalty to the group is absolute. Because they are inward-looking, such groups do not increase social capital in the broader community and their impact may be to limit opportunities for its creation. Not withstanding the need for an expression of diverse views within a society, activities that

create social capital are those that contribute to the 'common good', not the interest of a limited sector.

Definitions of social capital are still evolving. Some people emphasise the role of local organisations as sites for the development of social capital, while other writers, notably Cox, are interested in the potential for the creation of social capital across a range of relationships, from informal settings, such as between neighbours, to the role of trust and reciprocity in relationships between government and groups and individuals.

The concept of social capital is attractive to family workers for several reasons. Family workers put a lot of emphasis on developing networks. They offer families opportunities to expand their personal networks through running a wide range of formal and informal group activities. They also spend time nurturing relationships with the staff of other agencies. Because family workers work with families that may be facing a wide range of issues, they are likely to need effective working relationships across a very wide spectrum of organisations.

Family workers develop a close identification with the locality in which they are based. In a culturally diverse nation, the importance of respect for different cultural traditions and the value of employing staff from a range of traditions have been widely recognised. This means that a greater appreciation of cultural diversity and an active opposition to racism can develop both between families involved with agencies and between agency workers. The notion of creating social capital provides a framework within which to understand, and possibly start measuring, these activities.

American author Robert Putnam has helped foster interest in social capital. His work highlights the benefits of involvement in what he calls 'social organisations' or 'civic engagement' (Putnam, 1993). He sees this participation as important not only because of the achievement of individual groups but because of the impact that small-scale democracy can have on societies. Family workers have provided individuals who otherwise may have had little or no experience of such involvement with such opportunities. Participation on management or consultation committees, the opportunity to attend events such as annual general meetings and invitations to be involved in planning the family work program may not be available to family members anywhere else. Again, social capital provides a new window of understanding on such practices to which family workers have remained committed over many years, often in spite of suggestions that these are tokenistic or of little value compared to services provided directly to families.

Community building and Jen's family

Using an approach based on community building, Miriam decided that her work would focus on developing stronger links between Jen's family and other people in the area in which they live. These links will provide Jen with:

- a network of support
- opportunities to participate in making her community a better one.

As Miriam listened to Jen describing her experiences she was struck by Jen's isolation. Because Ron had not wanted her to spend time away from him, she had lost contact with friends. Her mother was dead, her sisters were interstate and preoccupied with their own children and concerns. Jen avoided contact with her neighbours, suspicious of anyone who would be desperate enough to live in the poorly maintained dwellings. Since Annie's preschool had notified the child protection service of their concerns she tried to avoid direct contact with the staff there as well, ducking in to collect Annie at the busiest times when she was least likely to be noticed. She had no one to talk to about her situation and no one to help her out with her immediate difficulties, such as child care while she was at work.

Miriam's approach was always to start with a family's most pressing concerns. But in the back of her mind she also started to think about ways in which she could encourage Jen and her children to take steps that could increase their sense of belonging in their neighbourhood. Jen's most pressing concern was that the child protection service might remove her children because they were being left alone at night. Jen's financial situation made it impossible for her to pay for child care, so Miriam suggested she try and renegotiate the repayment of her debts. At the centre where Miriam was based a financial counsellor held a session each week. Since Miriam's service had established a close working relationship with him, Miriam was able to arrange an urgent appointment for Jen. Although Jen was still liable for the debts, it was possible to negotiate reduced payments, and then Jen was able to work for a lower rate during the day. This reduced the tension between Jen and Lenny as he no longer had to be as responsible for Annie.

As Miriam spent time talking with Jen, it was evident that her relationship with Ron was still having a major impact on the family, even though they were no longer living together. Jen still had contact with Ron organising Annie's visits, and through this contact and her memories of his treatment of her, she felt she could never be free of Ron's shadow. When Miriam asked her if she would be interested in attending a group for women who were affected by domestic violence she was initially reticent. As she put it, she couldn't believe there could be anyone else alive who had such bad judgement in men. However, when she realised that Miriam would be involved in running the group, she said she would give it a go.

The group ran for a ten-week term. Jen was amazed to meet other women whose stories paralleled her own. Some of the women in the group were still living with their partners and one in particular was very interested in how Jen had managed to leave Ron. She had left her own partner but had gone back because she doubted her ability to cope alone. Jen was able to share her story and was surprised to find the other women in the group applauding what she had achieved. Even though she still went home to her depressing flat, she felt like a survivor rather than a failure.

She was even more surprised when she discovered that one of the women had a child at preschool with Annie. They arranged to take the children to the park together after preschool one day and Jen started to develop a friendship with someone who knew what she had been through. As Jen confessed to Miriam, what was most surprising was that her new friend Zita was Lebanese.

Jen had never had a friend who came from a different cultural background and, as she explained to Miriam, she had probably been pretty racist. But she'd felt really comfortable with Zita in the group and it was obvious they had a lot in common. Annie really enjoyed having a friend to play with outside preschool hours. Even Lenny hadn't complained when Jen tried out some recipes Zita had given her. In return she was able to help Zita out when Zita's baby was hospitalised.

As the group's meetings drew to a close, the women talked about how it had helped them. It occurred to them that, while they now had someone to talk to, many of their children had never had a chance to talk about what it was like living in a violent home. Encouraged by their comments, Miriam and her colleagues agreed to run two programs for children and young people who had been affected by domestic violence. Lenny and Annie attended the groups and although they didn't say much, Jen felt they seemed more relaxed than they had for a long time. Jen continued to find parenting Lenny hard work at times. Even when she no longer attended groups at the centre or saw Miriam regularly, she contacted her occasionally when she and Lenny were going through a rough patch. At one stage Miriam arranged for them to see an adolescent and family counsellor and Jen felt this enabled her to stop nagging Lenny, which helped.

Shortly after Jen began attending the domestic violence group at the family centre, Miriam passed on to her a pamphlet for the local community housing service. Although Jen wasn't very optimistic, she went to see them and was given priority because of the inadequate state of her current flat. Within several months she was able to move into a better flat at a cheaper rent. Although she was still cautious about getting to know her immediate neighbours, she was pleased that the new flat was not far from Zita's home.

While visiting the accommodation service to pay her rent, Jen saw a notice that the service needed volunteers to help with administration. She figured she could spare a few hours once a fortnight, especially as the housing service had contributed so much to her family. Although she found the work a bit daunting at first, she persisted and found she had an aptitude for figures. When Annie was a bit older she hoped that she would be able to do some formal study and find a job in bookkeeping.

Recently Jen was elected as a resident representative on the housing service management committee. She said that while she was pleased to be elected, the person who was most impressed was Lenny. She felt he didn't feel like he was living somewhere second class anymore because his mum was helping to run the show. When she looked back over the previous twelve months Jen commented that before she was alone on the outside. Now she knew that however tough it got from day to day, it was great to feel that she belonged somewhere.

OPTIMISM IN PRACTICE

As these versions of Jen's story illustrate, the four approaches are different. While each version highlights positive change, the means by which change occurs differ. There are differences in the way issues are brought to the foreground and in the resources accessed. Nevertheless, several shared themes emerge.

Each approach encourages the view that it is possible for individuals, families and communities to change. The process of change can be a challenging experience, with slip-ups and false starts along the way, and a belief in the possibility of change needs to be balanced with an awareness of the immediate needs of individual family members. In each version of Jen's story, for example, issues relating to the children's safety and supervision were identified and addressed. However, the underlying optimism that things do not have to stay as they are emerges clearly.

Within each approach the emphasis is on family or community direction rather than worker initiative. The capacity of family and community members to reflect on what works for them is respected. Because of this, in each approach there is an interest in looking for evidence of what has worked previously, and this can inform the present situation. The role of the worker is as a facilitator, or resource, but not as the ultimate authority on what family or community members must do.

In the next four chapters the approaches are explored in more depth. In the course of providing detailed description of the implementation of the approaches, each chapter identifies their influence on family work as it is practised. At the conclusion of each chapter, family members describe how change happened in their family.

three

Solution-focused work with families

Imagine that you are on holidays and you find a jigsaw puzzle. It's raining and cold outside and you figure that doing the puzzle would be a pleasant way to pass the afternoon. The only problem is that the box with the puzzle pieces doesn't have a lid. This means you have no picture to guide you as you put the pieces together. Nevertheless, you decide you would like a challenge. You empty all the pieces out of the box and start looking at them one by one. Half an hour later you feel alternately frustrated and foolish. You have found the four corner pieces, but you can't work out what the puzzle is supposed to look like. There are lots of green bits, and lots of black bits, but none of it makes sense. You think you might have found an eye, but you can't be sure. Various people have come to look at what you have been doing. One commiserates about how impossible jigsaws are. Someone else tells you about the jigsaw they half completed, only to discover that most of the rest of the pieces were missing. You feel like giving up. The more you look at all the little bits, the more confused you feel.

Staring at the shelf where you found the puzzle you see what looks like the lid of a box. You reach up, and discover that it is the lid of the jigsaw puzzle box. A large picture of a dinosaur is stuck to the top. Once you have seen the whole picture, you know where to start.

A solution-focused approach does not try to solve problems by examining them in detail. It places more importance on knowing what will be different when the problem is absent than on understanding the cause of the problem. The solution-focused approach emphasises what people are doing when the problem is absent, or less of a problem, rather than what people are doing wrong.

During life's normal ups and downs, people who start to slip into a deep decline are more likely to be noticed for what is going wrong for them than for everything else they are doing that is okay. A solution-focused approach suggests that an inappropriate and disproportionate amount of attention is given to the problem. Conversations become problem saturated. Not only does a person have a problem, they become the problem. This stops the person from seeing the solution. Other people start to provide answers and expect that their suggestions will be taken up. If they are, the person with the problem is at risk of becoming dependent on others to provide answers. They may view themselves as not coping and unable to manage without assistance. On the other hand, to reject the advice may leave them unsupported and labelled as resistant. A problem-saturated approach leads to discouragement and dependence.

A solution-focused approach would give priority to understanding the non-problem behaviour, the exceptions to the problem. This is informed by the belief that knowing more about what is driving the exceptional behaviour will provide the clues to choosing and creating behaviours that will be a part of the answer. Concentrating on what a person already does well nurtures confidence and hope. It focuses on the things that are already appropriate and useful. These provide the framework onto which new ideas and extra resources can be added.

A focus on solutions challenges the view that to change something that is a problem it is first necessary to find the cause and then attempt to fix it. Studies of human behaviour have found that people are not machines. There is no guarantee that even if you can identify the cause of the 'problem' that you can develop an absolute fix for it. Two people looking at the same behaviour can come up with quite different descriptions of the problem, the cause and the solution. Even if there is a direct link between the cause and the problem, this seldom indicates a direct solution.

Concerns have been identified about the parenting skills of Ali and Susan. One worker focuses on the lack of good parenting that Ali and Susan, both of whom were state wards, received. Another worker thinks that the problem is Susan's intellectual disability. Both of these descriptions of the problem relate to factors that cannot be changed.

A solution-focused approach offers an alternative to the view that there is one 'best' answer to a problem that can be found if family workers search hard enough. Instead it is assumed that there is always a range of possible solutions. Workers don't have to find the one right solution, they can construct one to fit. If a solution is tailor-made, it will be owned by the people who created it. This is important because what fits for one person won't fit for another. This approach suggests that perhaps when people feel that, in spite of all their efforts, things are going from bad to worse, it is because those who are trying to help persist in applying solutions that may have worked for others, but which don't fit for them.

Basic to the success of solution-focused practice is the worker's skill in listening and questioning. This is done in a style that validates the pain the person is experiencing while developing a sense of hope that things can be better.

The model presented here is one response to the challenge of constructing solutions. This solution-focused approach is a process rather than a theory. It first helps a family member decide what they want, looks for what is working and encourages the family member to do more of that. It then looks at what is not working and encourages the family member to do something different.

The worker's role involves demonstrating or modelling how solutions can be constructed, and assisting the family to implement the process for themselves. In the beginning this may mean doing things that, for the worker, seem insignificant in comparison to the problems the family members face. However, the solution-focused approach suggests that even small changes in behaviour can kick-start a process through which families can find out what works and do more of it, resulting in much bigger changes further down the track.

Nadia and Chris's family are confronting a huge range of issues. They are behind on their rent, their fourteen-year-old son is faced with criminal charges related to theft, Nadia's mother is very sick and there are disputes with the neighbours. The family worker, Mark, tries to look at solutions with Nadia and Chris. To Mark's surprise, Nadia and Chris identify that having the family dog desexed is a high priority for action. Mark assists them in the process of finding a cheap vet and with them develops a plan to save up for the fee which must be payed in advance. The change in the dog's behaviour following the operation has an immediate impact on relationships with the neighbours. Following the success of the short-term saving plan, Nadia and Chris start to see the possibilities for creating a longer term budget to ensure that their rent is paid on time and that their son has regular pocket money.

BECOMING A SOLUTION FINDER

1 Believing that people have strengths and capabilities to solve problems

The solution-focused approach is based on the belief that people have the strength and capability to solve problems. The techniques that support the approach cannot be applied if the worker is operating from pessimistic assumptions about the family's capacity to construct solutions. If the worker believes that people have the strengths and capabilities that are needed, they will be wary about giving advice or directing people to solutions that have worked for others. They will also accept that family members are experts on their own situation. As a result they will be prepared to work with the family on solution strategies that may be very different from what they would personally have chosen to do because they accept that the family needs to own the solutions for them to work.

> Jackie discusses with a family worker the problems she has with home management. This is impacting on her two children because they are going to school in smelly clothes and being ridiculed. Jackie has identified that a solution will involve the children having clean clothes to wear each day. She decides that this can happen if she goes to the second-hand store and buys eight sets of clothes for each child and takes a big load to the laundry once a week to be washed and dried.

The central guide to practice within a solution-focused approach is an emphasis on the family members' capacities to create solutions in the present that can grow into the future, rather than on the worker's experience of how problems have been addressed in the past.

2 Developing a picture of what will replace 'doing the problem'

In early contact with the family, the worker needs to find out what the family want from their contact with the service. There are many ways to do this depending on the opportunities presented by the family.

Family workers engage with people who feel extremely uncomfortable with some aspect of their lives. Sometimes family workers will meet families who have been directed to them by a statutory authority. These family members may feel as if they have not had a real choice. Regardless of how they contact the service, families have the right to expect that they will be received respectfully and offered an opportunity to work on solutions to their own issues.

Few will come to the service with a clear picture of how they want things to be. They are more likely to be able to describe what is not working. The weight of the problem is blinding them from seeing beyond it. The workers need to listen to their stories of discouragement and acknowledge their grief, pain and confusion. This does not mean joining them in the problem. Instead the workers join families in developing a picture of what they will be doing when the problem is not dominating. What will replace 'doing the problem'? More often than not this picture of the future will include doing more of what already works.

> Marie, a sixteen-year-old, and her parents came for assistance because her school was concerned that she was suicidal. After hearing accounts of the parents' shock and fear and their daughter's sadness, the worker and the family together began to build two pictures. The first was a detailed picture of the young woman's behaviours and her parents' and others' responses on bad days, when she felt picked on and worthless. The second was a very clear picture of her behaviour and others' responses on good days, when she felt able to cope and even risked being happy. In the very act of building this second picture the tone of the interview changed considerably. A 'blanket' had been lifted. This was the picture Marie wanted to see more often.

The clearer the picture, the easier it is to recreate. Sometimes it will include behaviours and feelings that will be new, but usually such behaviours are not so new that family members do not have a realistic vision of themselves enacting that behaviour.

If family members are feeling overwhelmed by the problem to

the extent that they are unable to develop an alternative picture to the problem behaviour, they may feel that the worker does not appreciate the difficulties of their situation. They may see being asked to imagine a different picture as an indication that the worker thinks they need to 'think positive'. It is important to validate the family members' experiences and acknowledge the hurt before moving on to some different ways of building the solution picture.

Sometimes families can still feel stuck in the problem situation, even after their experience has been validated. Some strategies to deal with this include:

- *Leaving the family with a 'homework' task:* A worker says to a family, 'Between now and when I see you again, I would like you to notice the things that happen that you would like to do more of or have happen more often.'
- *Using the 'Miracle Question':* A worker says to a family, 'You go to bed tonight and, without you knowing it, a miracle happens. When you wake up in the morning, your problem has been solved. What will you be doing differently?'

  The Miracle Question helps develop a hypothetical picture that can stand outside the family member's immediate experience of the problem behaviour. It provides an excuse to look beyond the heaviness of the now. It is important that families don't feel as if their concerns are being trivialised when the Miracle Question is being introduced. The worker needs to communicate respect for the family and the reality of their situation.

  The Miracle Question often works well because by its very nature it assumes that the family member does not have to know about how to solve the problem to know what it will be like when the problem is solved. For some people it is easier to imagine how they will feel once the problem is solved and then to allow that to help develop the picture of doing the solution. In many circumstances it is useful to add to the question so that it becomes 'What will you be feeling and doing differently?'

On occasions the family member's picture of the future will be unrealistic or unattainable by legal methods. For example, a person might desire a cure for a person with a terminal illness or they might imagine that they have murdered their child's abuser. Although these miracles might be unlikely to happen and, as in the latter case, they might not be advisable, the feelings that would be present if these things did happen can be explored and alternative ways of reaching these feelings can be investigated.

The purpose of strategies such as the Miracle Question is to focus on what people would do when the problem is absent. The clarity of the picture of the desired behaviour is critical. The family member needs to be able to see themselves doing the different or new behaviour. The clearer the vision of the behaviour in action, the more confident the family member will feel about being able to achieve that behaviour. In some ways the picture provides the opportunity to practise.

> Jay is working with the Taylor family. They are finding it hard to develop a picture of what things would be like when the problem that has led them to seek help from Jay has gone. Each family member has their version of how unpleasant the family relation-ships are and who they see as responsible for this. However, the family has told Jay of a meal they shared during the week that did not end in a fight. Jay says, 'Imagine if I snuck into your kitchen with a hidden video camera and took a film of that meal. When we sat down together to view the video, what would we see?' Gradually the family is able to build up a picture of people letting others finish conversations, not criticising each other and planning family treats together.

3 Doing more of what is working now or has worked in the past

Once family members have a clear picture of what they want to be doing, the desired picture, it is possible to identify the current be-haviours that work, that are a part of the desired picture. These behaviours can then be encouraged.

It is extremely rare that the problem behaviour is happening all the time, every minute of the day. By identifying the non-problem behaviour, the exceptions to the problem, the family members iden-tify what works and what they want to do more of. Doing more of what works has many benefits. It confirms that the person is not the problem, highlights coping behaviour and develops confidence to move on. By achieving some quality time, free from the stress created by the problem, people have space to think about new ideas and behaviours. It also leaves family members with better resources to cope with the times when the problem does dominate, and encour-ages family members to take control of the change process.

Much work with families has emphasised the importance of

assessment. Assessment has involved developing a detailed understanding of the family's problems, their origins, history and influence. Solution-focused work concentrates on getting a better understanding of the exceptions. Practitioners of this approach want to know what is happening when the problem is not occurring. Life's natural course is one of ups and downs. If a person drops too deeply into a down, it is difficult to remember how to get up. An assessment of the exception helps remind people about the skills they have used in the past to get back up. These skills and the context in which they were used can be recreated or adapted to assist in the new dilemma.

> Karen has hit her baby. The worker asks her, 'How often have you felt this way before, but not hit your baby?'

Being weighed down by the problem can make it difficult to think about the exceptions to the problem behaviour. If a family member is unable to identify something they are doing that is working and that is helping them to cope, introducing scaling may help. Scaling encourages people to see the problem behaviour as being on a continuum. At different points in time there will be more or less of the problem behaviour happening. Scaling takes many different forms but the simplest is probably the notion of a line numbered one to ten.

> Rhani is having difficulty identifying exceptions to her experience of her life being out of control. After listening to her carefully, the worker asks her, 'On a scale of one to ten, where would you place yourself today on that scale, where one means having no control and ten means being totally in control?' She places herself at three. The worker then asks, 'What are you doing now that is stopping you from slipping further back down the scale?' Rhani starts to talk about the fact that at least she was able to keep her arrangement to meet with the family worker. This provides an opportunity to explore the ways that Rhani has exercised control over her life.

If the family member has a view of themselves as the problem rather than as the person doing the problem or caught in the problem behaviour, the technique of externalising will be useful. Externalising places the person in the situation rather than describing the person in a way that portrays them as the problem.

> Kate says, 'I'm weak, I just give in every time he starts yelling at me.' The worker responds, 'When he starts yelling, you feel you have no power to put your point of view. The yelling takes control.'

The family worker and family members can identify opportunities to practise doing more of what works. Part of this process includes deciding how to measure the success of this practise.

> Margie says, 'Next time he won't listen to my point of view, I'll remember to say to myself, "Well, it's his loss if he makes mistakes and has to start all over again," and I'll walk out of the room.' The worker asks Margie how she will know if this is successful. Margie decides to note how many times when she does this her partner comes to her for her advice.

Measuring can work in a number of ways. It helps people notice what works and what else changes at the same time. For example, people often find that as they do things differently, their feelings become more positive and optimistic. Measuring can put reversions to unwanted behaviour in context, so that people can see that reversions are normal and are simply reminders to do more of what works.

4 Adding on new behaviour

Once the family have a clear picture of the desired future and have clarified which parts of current behaviour they wish to highlight in the future picture, the worker can assist by helping them identify the parts of the behaviour that are not working. Sometimes these behaviours will get in the way of reaching the desired picture of the future. In this case family members might choose to develop new behaviours or skills that will help them to avoid pitfalls in the future. These new behaviours can be added in a style that complements the useful known behaviours.

The worker's role at this stage is to help family members identify what is needed to do things differently. By encouraging the family to reflect on the existing strengths and skills they use in other contexts, the worker can assist the family to identify strengths and skills that might assist them to find or ask for the necessary resources.

At times a family member will not recognise how one already well-developed skill could facilitate the acquiring of another. A worker would have a legitimate role in helping family members make these connections and see how skills are transposable. Telling alone will not work. The worker needs to open up conversations that allow family members to discover this themselves.

> Mara's skill in managing to budget on a low income reflects the process that she could use to plan a staged escape from a violent

partner. She knows about timing, prioritising and negotiating. The worker starts to assist her to make these links. The worker asks, 'I wonder if there is something else you do like budgeting, for example, that might give some clues to thinking about how to plan this?'

Mara responds, 'What do you mean?'

The worker replies, 'Well, I've always admired your ability to think about what you need and to juggle your bills and other purchases.'

When the family members have done everything they can for themselves, the worker may have a role in advocating on their behalf. This may be because a particular agency validates the perception of workers' judgements, but not of families, or because family members are exhausted and can do no more. Depending on the circumstances, the family's observations of the worker advocating on their behalf may assist them in developing new skills and behaviour when they need to access resources on their own in the future.

A family may need information to develop new skills. Choices are limited by the information available. Once the family feels fairly sure about what they want to do differently, a worker can help them access the relevant information.

Voula and Con feel worn out by constant battles with their child who is a poor eater. Their extended family constantly remark on the limited range of foods he will eat. Their picture of what they want to do differently includes relaxed mealtimes with time to talk. Information about dietary requirements assists them to put this different behaviour into practice without being overwhelmed by anxiety that their child's health will suffer.

Families may need access to resources outside the family and the family work service to make their picture of the desired future a reality.

Bette has decided she wants a non-violent household for her family. She uses legal advice and access to emergency accommodation and financial support to achieve this. She and her children also use specialised group work to assist them in establishing a non-violent future.

Simple planning tools can facilitate the process of enacting new behaviours and help the focus stay on solutions. Such tools assist a family to follow a process of solution finding as they put on paper the steps in this process. These tools work best when they are adapted for the particular circumstances facing the family.

> Lily, the family worker, sits down with the Clint family as they create a chart. Lily has had two previous conversations with the family as they have sought assistance with the tension created by the recent refusal of twelve-year-old Sacha to attend family functions. Lily draws up five columns on a big sheet of butchers' paper. She explains that in the first column they should write down the specific goal they want to work on. After some animated discussion the Clints decide to focus on having family activities that they can all enjoy together. Lily asks Sacha to write this in the first column. Lily then heads up the remaining columns with:
>
> • examples of family activities that have been enjoyable in the past
> • what made those times enjoyable?
> • specific tasks to ensure the next family activity is enjoyable— who has to do what?
> • what will it be like for us when a family activity is enjoyable for everyone?
>
> By the end of the planning session, the Clints have worked out that they will be enjoying family activities together when everyone has a say in what and when activities will be held, and when Sacha is given the opportunity to bring friends with her from time to time.

SOLUTION-FOCUSED WORK AND CHILD PROTECTION

While a solution-focused approach encourages workers to be optimistic about the possibilities, regardless of the problem, the context within which this work is done must be acknowledged. For some families this context includes the involvement of statutory child protection services because of concerns about the safety or wellbeing of the children. Family workers using solution-focused ideas recognise the importance of discussing these concerns explicitly with families from the beginning. In some situations immediate intervention, such as placement of the child outside the home, is necessary. Removing children in itself does little more than create immediate safe refuge. It is not a solution to the situation that created the danger. However, placement can be one strategy that provides time for a plan to be made.

Where there is a high level of concern regarding safety, protective workers and the courts may set a 'bottom line', which should set out clearly what the family are expected to do if a child is to remain in or return to their care. For example, the bottom line might be that a person whose violent behaviour has led to a child being harmed needs to move out of the home. The family, not the workers, are responsible for ensuring that they comply with the bottom line. The bottom line can be another strategy for providing the time to develop solutions. During this time it may be the role of the family worker to develop a partnership with family members, assisting them to work on solutions of their choice that allow them to demonstrate to themselves and the protective services their constructive contribution to their child's safe future.

While statutory intervention can be a necessary part of ensuring the safety of children, it can contribute to family members feeling even more powerless and pessimistic about their situation. The solution-focused approach addresses this by actively involving the family in the development of a plan. The role of the family worker will depend on the work already done by protective workers and others. The family worker might be involved in all or any of the stages of solution-focused work: helping family members to decide what they want, encouraging them to do more of what is working and assisting them to develop new behaviours.

> The Pringle family identify their goal as wanting to live together without the statutory authorities playing a role in their life. Their goal also includes living somewhere clean and comfortable, with the parents feeling more relaxed and able to cope, and the children not having fighting and yelling around them. The family recalls times in the past when the children were safe in the care of the family and discuss them in detail, looking for hints that might make it possible to repeat this. The Pringles then organise some practice tasks to use during access visits.

The solution-focused approach can be implemented alongside the statutory processes of child protection. For example, once the family has some ideas about the things they are going to do, these can be shared with protective services workers. They can form part of the plan that is developed to ensure the children's safety. Often statutory processes include the use of formal meetings to develop and review plans. The family's ideas about the behaviours they want to see more of and the strategies they want to use can be presented at the meetings. The statutory plan can then reflect the family's ideas and language, which can give them a real sense of involvement in and ownership of the process. A planning chart can be used to provide a structure for formal meetings. This ensures that the family's ideas are not swamped by the contributions of other workers, and that the focus of the meeting is on what can be done differently to meet the children's needs, rather than on what the family have done wrong.

After a plan has been developed, review sessions can receive feedback on the family's discoveries about what works. These sessions may draw together the family with the range of workers who have been involved with them.

Scaling tools can be used to keep track of changes. While recognising the reality of child protection concerns, focusing attention on what works encourages the family to persist in their efforts to do things differently and allows workers to gain a clear picture about what is being done differently.

Family workers involved in child protection work emphasise the need to be open to the family's ideas, rather than relying on workers' ideas about the best way to achieve goals. Because the family members are experts on their own situation, they may be able to find quite unconventional ways of doing things. The key question is not whether anyone else has tried this solution before, but what leads the family members to feel that this way can work for them and contribute to their children's safety.

> Judi found it hard to get her children up and ready for school in the morning. She decided to get her children to wear their school tracksuits to bed, rather than conventional pyjamas. The next morning they were able to get ready much faster and she could get them to school on time.

From time to time families may find some aspects of the solution plan do not work in the way they had hoped. This could mean that children are again harmed or exposed to situations where they are at risk. These situations must be acknowledged, but the way that this is done can have a major impact on the family's capacity to continue in the solution-building process. The kind of language used can be significant. While that language should not minimise the impact of what has happened to the child, it may be more useful in many situations to talk about 'challenges' or 'slip-ups' than of 'making mistakes' or 'doing the wrong thing'.

If the statutory authorities need to be advised, the family worker may encourage the family to take this step, rather than taking over the process. Such a step is also dependent on the family's capacity to act and the family worker's assessment of the statutory authority's capacity to respond to the information in a way that puts the family's action in a helpful context. For example, if the statutory authorities assume that because the family has reported the incident themselves, there is not really a problem, the family's struggles and the child's needs might not be addressed.

Recent experience and research in child welfare supports the view that it is almost always in the best interests of children for their family to be actively involved in their future, regardless of the outcome of statutory intervention (Farmer and Owen 1995). The solution-focused approach can engage family members in what can be done, rather than emphasising what can't.

SOLUTION-FOCUSED WORK AND DOMESTIC VIOLENCE

In theory there is no reason why the assumptions on which a solution-focused approach is based should not be applied to work with families where there is domestic violence. In practice, however, when workers are confronted with the impact of violence it may be very difficult to believe that members of the family do have the capacity to identify and construct solutions. If the worker feels that the 'solution' that family members have chosen is in fact exposing them to further violence, there is an even greater challenge.

However, workers who have actively used solution-focused ideas report that they can be effective in assisting at least some family members to take active steps for change in their lives. At the same time they acknowledge that there will also be times when family members make choices that, at least in the immediate future, workers find hard to accept and may not be able to support.

Often when family workers are addressing issues of domestic violence they are primarily working with female partners. Because of concerns about the efficacy of working with couples where there is violence, some agencies have formal or informal protocols that limit their involvement with perpetrators. In other situations the female partner is the one who has been referred or is seeking assistance. In some cases the violence may have precipitated a self-referral or resulted in intervention from the police or child protection service. Sometimes family members may mention violence, but see it as peripheral to other issues. The decision about whether to work primarily with those who are recipients of violence or to consider an approach that includes some sessions with all family members will depend on the worker's judgement about whether the safety of family members, in particular children, will be compromised. Such decisions will also be influenced by agency policy regarding work with perpetrators of violence.

The starting point for solution-focused work involves hearing the family's story and assisting family members to draw a picture of how they would like things to be different. At this point family members might identify a life without violence as part of their picture. Although it can be very tempting at this stage for family workers to prescribe ways in which this could be achieved, such as leaving the perpetrator of the violence, both experience and the assumptions underlying the solution-focused approach suggest that such advice is unlikely to be an effective strategy. Leaving a relationship is likely to be a challenging and even dangerous undertaking. To do this successfully requires ownership of the decision, which can encourage persistence when the going gets tough. It is also important to recognise that it is inappropriate for a worker to put themselves in a role through which they are replacing the perpetrator of violence as the controlling force in the family. Workers emphasise that, realistically, it can take time for a woman to explore whether it is possible to find ways of having a non-violent life and remaining with her partner.

Some women may return to that partner several times in the process of leaving. This can be challenging for workers who are concerned for the safety of the woman and her children. It is understandable that sometimes workers feel critical of women in this situation. They might even be compelled to share their perception that the woman has made a mistake. If the woman is feeling stuck between two impossible alternatives or apprehensive about what she should do, such comments might make it harder for her to talk openly with the worker. Even where the worker finds it hard to see a woman's actions as a solution, it can still be helpful to explore how the woman sees them as contributing to the picture she wants to do more of.

A dilemma for workers assisting families affected by domestic violence arises around questions of responsibility. Sometimes questions about what people would be doing differently if life were free of violence can give greater clarity to questions of responsibility. Such questions can enable family members to confront a more realistic picture about their own behaviour and responsibility. They can clarify the distinction between being responsible for making a contribution toward peace in the household while not being responsible for a partner's violent actions.

Jillian describes an incident where she raised a contentious issue with her partner without his becoming violent. She comments on the fact that she did not nag or pressure her partner, but instead left the issue to be resolved later. She says, 'If I had nagged, I would have set off the violence.'

The family worker asks, 'If your life was free of violence, how would you communicate with your partner?'

Jillian thinks hard about this and answers, 'Well, I wouldn't pressure him, but I would feel safe to give my opinion.'

While there can be a fine line at times between giving information and prescribing solutions, workers report that it can be helpful to give recipients of violence information that can assist family members in thinking about what will replace 'doing the problem' and what family members are doing at times when the home is free from violence. This could include information about community values regarding women's rights to be safe and to live free from violence, and about the consequences of violence for children. Information about developing safety plans can be valuable as a strategy for women to prepare to do something different when violence occurs.

SOLUTION-FOCUSED WORK AND FAMILIES LIVING IN POVERTY

The solution-focused approach suggests that there is always a range of possible solutions that could be constructed to address a problem. Yet family workers will be aware that for families with limited access to money, possibilities are inevitably constrained and the impact of living in poverty will make it harder to implement solutions. Unemployment, money worries, inadequate housing and lack of transport, for example, all have an impact on the possibilities available to the family and on the family's sense of optimism that things can be different. Sometimes this means that workers become so conscious of the choices that family members are not able to make, they find it hard to be open to different or unexpected possibilities.

Because a solution-focused approach makes a clear distinction between the person and the problem, using solution-focused ideas can help families to look at what could be different without their being overwhelmed by a sense of blame or stigma. While solution-focused work does not seek to explain or analyse social and economic forces, once people are less preoccupied with self-blame or unworthiness, they will be better able to think about the exceptions in their life and more ready to identify what they are doing that they would like to do more of.

Although solution-focused work looks to expand the family's idea of how things can be different, the path toward a different situation must be grounded in the family's day-to-day life, not merely in slogans. As families develop a clearer picture of desirable behaviour and look for ways to do this more, there will be constraints on their choices and resources, especially where financial resources are limited. Acknowledging these limitations can help families to see more clearly what they can influence and what they cannot. This can assist them to use their energy on strategies that are realistic and feasible.

Family workers who use solution-focused ideas have found they can apply them not just to work with individuals and families, but also to larger scale issues. Finding what works and doing more of it can be valuable in developing strategies for advocating for families on specific issues and also for building broader coalitions. The notion that understanding problems does not necessarily lead to generating effective solutions can be applied as readily to thinking about inequality as it can to issues for individual families. Solution-focused approaches enable workers to think not just about what factors promote inequality, but about what kinds of policies and practice promote equity.

> Staff at Bushland Family Services became aware of families on limited incomes in financial difficulties because of the high interest rates they are paying on loans for essential household appliances such as washing machines. The staff talked a great deal about the injustice of the system of credit and then they posed the Miracle Question: 'What would it be like if the credit system was just?' They pictured a society where families on low incomes had the opportunity to apply for affordable credit. This led them to set up a no interest loan scheme.

CHALLENGES FOR WORKERS USING SOLUTION-FOCUSED IDEAS

Believing that the family has the strength and capability to solve problems

The commonsense nature and the apparent simplicity of solution-focused ideas are very appealing to many workers who chose their profession because of their commitment to seeing all people receive a fair deal. Because it is family member directed and hence respectful, it matches many family workers' vision of acting in partnership with family members, rather than coming from a position of knowing best. Persisting with solution-focused practice, however, requires a considerable amount of discipline. The worker has not only to accept that the family has the strength and capability to solve ideas, but has to hold these as an integral part of their belief system. Without this commitment, workers may find themselves going back to more familiar or comfortable patterns of working when times become tough, practices that emphasise the worker's competence rather than the family's. It can take time for workers to develop the confidence to persist with a belief in the family's capacity and to be open to solutions that may not fit with accepted wisdom about what works.

Joint work or discussion with other people using a similar approach can be very helpful when workers feel their beliefs about the possibility of change are wavering or when they find themselves paying more attention to problems than solutions. Of course, if workers really feel they cannot believe in the family's capacity to solve problems, they need to be cautious. Their perception that the approach cannot work at that time will obstruct constructive action, and the family may feel as though they have been set up. Before that point workers might find it helpful to question themselves about their doubts. Sometimes it is the concerns of others, including other agencies working from a different set of beliefs, that challenge the worker, rather than what the family members have said or done. Where workers are part of a solution-focused team they can draw on the strengths and experience of colleagues who share their beliefs about change.

Making discoveries, not telling people what they do well

It is important that family members identify competencies for themselves. The worker's role is to facilitate this, not to tell family members what they do well. Telling can be experienced as condescending and is often unconvincing. If the family member is feeling hopeless, they may not really believe the worker. Asking questions rather than making statements about a family member's achievements makes it easier for workers to avoid the temptation of trying to convince a family member that they have done something well or different. For example, rather than making a statement such as, 'You've done a really good job there', a worker might ask, 'How did you do that?' or 'What were you doing differently?'

Once the family member learns a process of self-discovery the same process can be used at other times. Subsequently, family members are less likely to become dependent on the worker's presence and better prepared to persist in constructing solutions even in the face of obstacles.

Solution-focused work may not be brief

The development of solution-focused ideas was strongly influenced by brief therapy approaches to families and individuals. As its name suggests, brief therapy assumes that more is not necessarily better and that effective intervention can consist of quite short-term intervention. Family workers using solution-focused ideas may work with some families over only a few weeks. However, in other situations, especially where there are child protection concerns or the family is dealing with a range of complicated issues, contact between the worker and the family may extend over some months. It may include many more sessions than the six to ten that are often associated with brief therapy. During this time family workers would often address a wide range of issues, including practical problems that more formal therapy programs would not address. Developing links with other services, finding new friends, sorting out complex legal or financial problems, or relocating to a new home or a new neighbourhood could all be part of assisting a family to do what will replace the problem.

While an agency's work with a family might continue over some time, this could be seen as a series of brief contacts. This allows for recognition of the family's progressive achievements, and enables the family and the worker to have a clear focus on the current goals. The challenge is to ensure that in the process family members continue to identify and build on their own strengths, rather than increasing their reliance on the worker's strengths. Regularly reviewing progress with the family and ensuring a continuing focus on the family's capacities can assist workers to avoid inadvertently encouraging dependence.

Respecting diverse solutions and strategies

The solutions generated by family members will be coloured by their beliefs and experiences. Families from diverse cultural backgrounds may identify quite different solutions that reflect particular cultural perspectives. This may prove challenging for a family worker whose own experiences and values might lead them to favour quite different options.

For example, a family might accept or even welcome a degree of involvement by their extended family that to a worker could seem overly authoritarian or paternalistic. While the worker may explore with the family the advantages and disadvantages of different options, the focus needs to be on the experience of family members, not on the beliefs of the family worker. This may involve the worker seeking the guidance of the family or of someone who shares the family's cultural background to help them to appreciate and respect the cultural values informing the options that the family selects.

While the solution-focused approach's emphasis on the family's ideas provides space for cultural beliefs to be respected in the development of solutions, practices that are associated with solution-focused work may be strongly influenced by particular culturally determined beliefs. For example, brainstorming—generating a list of possibilities without worrying about finding the right answer first off—assumes that family members are comfortable putting forward ideas that may be contradictory. Round-table brainstorming may, on the surface, give all family members a voice in decision making, which could be seen as challenging culturally accepted beliefs about the role of men or the role of older people in the family.

Family workers using a solution-focused approach would generally try to avoid giving advice, preferring instead to ask questions and encourage the exploration of possibilities. This could be confusing for families whose expectation is that someone who is competent will be able to provide answers. Using questions to open up discussion could have quite the opposite effect for family members who assume that it would be disrespectful not to give the answers expected of them. They may try to second-guess the worker's expectations or they may feel safer not answering at all.

These challenges do not disqualify a solution-focused approach in an environment of cultural diversity. Instead, they draw attention to the importance of family workers seeking to set aside their own cultural baggage and working with families in a way that fits with the family's needs and beliefs.

LIKE BABY STEPS: DEBBIE'S STORY

Debbie is a sole parent now living in a small rural town. Her children were removed by the child welfare authorities because they were being physically abused by her former partner. Her story illustrates that:

- identifying causes is not a prerequisite for change
- there is a difference between setting goals for people and assisting them to set their own goals
- visualising how things will be different without the problem assists families.

> We were so far out of town, I couldn't get to the services. In the end the only way I could get help was to send the boys to school with bruises all over them and pray someone would listen. But they took them away.
>
> I was full of hate towards the welfare department. I didn't want to know why they took them. I thought, 'What's the point of me showing anything to anyone? They're not going to let my kids come home.' I was the type of person who knew everything but knew nothing.
>
> It was scary with family support at first. I thought they wouldn't want to know what I was. They used a column approach. Instead of being one huge thing to look at, it's broken down. I've got to put down my ideas, what my goals are, and what I've got to do to get from one position to another. It meant actually seeing what I had to do to achieve my goals. If someone had come to me and said, 'You have to do this, this, this and then you'll get this as your goal', it would just go in but it wouldn't sink in. You make your own decisions about what to put on it. I could look at it and say, 'I can get from there to there'. My starting point was that I was suicidal and I wanted to get out of being suicidal. Then I wanted to see my kids. After that I wanted to have full-time access and from access I wanted to have the kids returned. I had to give up the relationship with the abuser. I had to prove to my kids that I was there as a

mother for them and I had to show them here was a safe place. It's meant being there for my kids where before medication was more important to me, having medication and not worrying what the kids were up to.

I've made one of my goals. It's taken fifteen months, but one of my sons will be home soon. It's worked with one and we're getting the access going with the other one so I can see a change with him as well. My daughter has come back from living with my mother. She's returned to me too.

I've had to have a lot of contact with the welfare department. Fighting like I was before got nowhere. I don't get angry with them, I don't yell and scream. I'm on a working level with them. They keep telling me I'm a changed person and that makes me feel proud. I can sit back and say I've worked with those people to get my kids.

I've become more aware of abusive situations with my kids. I think I've become a lot more courageous. I can stand up and tell someone what I think now instead of cowering down and being a wimp. I think the hardest thing when my son comes back will be dealing with his temper tantrums. But now I can turn around and say, 'No, you're not having it'. Before I'd say, 'Go to your room' and then I'd go and say 'I'm sorry'.

Now I can send him to his room and say, 'Stay, and then we'll talk'. It was like baby steps all over again. I was lost, but now I'm a found person. It was like climbing Mt Everest without a rope but I've finally made it. What kept me going was seeing the smiles on my kids' faces and knowing they were proud of who I am now.

FINDING OUT MORE

The solution-focused approach built on ideas from brief therapy, which emphasised the importance of addressing the things that maintain problems, rather than what causes them. The work of Steve de Shazar has been significant in the development of interest in solutions as something quite distinct from the understanding of problems. While de Shazar's original ideas were developed in clinical settings, in which a therapist and a family met for appointments in an office, other practitioners—notably Insoo Kim Berg—have extended the use of these ideas to a range of more informal settings.

Berg, Insoo Kim (1994) *Family Based Services: A Solution-Focused Approach*, W.W. Norton, New York. Berg outlines how a solution-focused approach can be used in work with families where there are child protection concerns.

De Shazar, Steve (1985) *Keys to Solution in Brief Therapy*, W.W. Norton, New York. This book discusses the significance of a focus on the solution rather than the problem and identifies the implications of this in practice.

Scott, Dorothy, and O'Neil, Di (1998) *Beyond Child Rescue*, Solution Press, Victoria. The work of St Luke's, a family and community service organisation that provides a range of services throughout North Central Victoria, is described with details of the approaches and tools St Luke's staff have developed to engage families and others in the process of identifying strengths and noticing change.

four

Narrative approach to working with families

Imagine you are discussing a movie that you have seen with a group of friends. You have all seen the same film, but what has struck each person might be quite different. One person describes a character as a hero, while someone else says he was misguided. You recount what you thought was the high point, but someone else suggests that a different scene was more important. Everyone has seen the same film, but the accounts of it are all different. Some people are particularly forceful in arguing their point. You might have thought the plot was a bit weak, but they will not rest until they have convinced you that you have seen a masterpiece.

The narrative approach suggests that, just as there may be competing accounts of one movie, the story of a person's life can be told in very different ways. It all depends on the perspective. A person will pick out some incidents as significant and leave others aside. They will highlight some of their feelings and bypass others. This process is going on constantly and most of the time people are barely aware of it.

Hearing the family's story is always an important part of family work. In narrative work, the worker will be listening carefully. This is not just to find out who are the important people in the family and what have been the significant events. The worker will also be listening to discover how people make sense of it all.

> A family worker is talking to Maria, who is discussing life with her three-year-old Todd. As the family worker hears the blow-by-blow description of Todd's latest misdemeanour, she is also noting the words Maria uses and the recurring theme that nothing about parenting is what she expected. The worker is listening for explanations and ideas about how and why things happened. She is paying attention to aspects of the story that are highlighted and to those that are barely mentioned.

Families do not develop accounts of their lives in a vacuum. The worker listens to find out about the family's particular context, and the wider cultural and social influences. The narrative approach draws on the idea that within society certain accounts or 'dominant' stories are very powerful. These stories express commonly accepted ideas that are rarely questioned. They are given a status of being 'the truth'. However, these stories vary from community to community. Different societies will have different dominant stories.

The everyday or accepted language with which people describe particular events or experiences is never neutral. It carries with it associations that shape people's beliefs and experiences as they speak. Dominant stories often include a preoccupation with blame and guilt. They may include assumptions that events should have been predicted and avoided, and that particular individuals should have been in control. Other themes can include the cataloguing of weaknesses and deficiencies.

> The Brent family is known among many local community agencies as a multi-problem family. When seventeen-year-old Sally Brent turns up to a support group for pregnant teenagers, the worker reports back to her colleague 'like mother, like daughter'.

Such comments fail to acknowledge the economic and social context that has influenced the lives of families such as Sally's. They also fail to consider the extraordinary ability of families to stick together in spite of tremendous challenges, their ability to survive under adverse circumstances and the aspirations they have for themselves and their children.

One characteristic effect of dominant stories is often to emphasise the legitimacy of the knowledge of recognised 'experts' who analyse and classify the situation. This tendency reduces the attention paid to grassroots or 'local' knowledge that focuses on unique individual situations. Consequently people with concerns or difficulties might be encouraged to look for solutions from experts and assume that their own understanding of their situation must be deficient.

> Bob is a new parent who bought a book about baby care at the newsagent. He is at his wits' end about his and his wife Sonia's inability to settle their crying baby. The book sets out a five-step plan to establish a sleep routine for the baby. Bob and his wife see their inability to put this plan into practice as confirmation that their parenting is at fault, rather than considering the possibility that the five-step program does not fit with their family's situation.

The narrative approach suggests that the effect of dominant stories is to limit the options available for people to make sense of their experience. Dominant stories encourage people to explain situations within a narrow range of preconceived ideas. This also affects people's ability to access resources and strategies for achieving change.

Narrative work aims to open up the space for accounts of people's lives that fit better with their lived experience. These preferred stories may allow people to notice and see as important aspects of their experience that have been overlooked before. The new stories invite changes to the kind of language people use to talk about their experience.

> Bob and Sonia request help with parenting from a family worker. The family worker highlights their commitment to parenting and their ability to recognise their child's responses. This helps Bob and Sonia to see themselves as competent parents, who may need to experiment to find the most effective strategy to settle their baby.

OPENING SPACE FOR PREFERRED STORIES

1 Listening

This kind of listening requires the worker to put aside beliefs and preconceptions that focus on the worker's interpretation of the story. Family workers are not immune to the influence of dominant stories, whether they are generated within the wider community or among themselves. Instead of listening for information about what is wrong with the family, within the narrative approach the worker is listening for what things mean for the family. This means putting aside the expectation that the worker can know things about the family that the family do not know about themselves. This approach does not assume that the worker can predict what is going to be significant and should therefore steer discussion with the family in those directions. Providing such direction can have a significant impact on history taking and assessment. Narrative workers therefore take a stance of being a 'bit behind the family' as opposed to being 'beyond the family'.

At the same time the context in which family work is practised demands that issues such as the safety of children must be part of the conversations. The narrative approach does not mean that workers only discuss the topics raised by families. There are many situations where agency protocol, developed in response to the agency's purpose and mission, requires workers to explore particular issues with families.

> A worker meets a family where there is a young child who is very small for her age. The family is focused on a dispute with the owner of their rented accommodation. While the worker links the family with a tenancy advice service, he also starts a conversation with the family about what they enjoy about their daughter and areas in which they find parenting her a challenge. The parents talk about the child as a fussy eater and the contradictory advice they have received about how to deal with that.

The worker's priority is to listen for the family's construction of meaning, rather than taking a stance of 'expert-knowing'. Expert-knowing fits what the family says into what the worker already knows. This stance may have led the worker in the previous example to begin by asking the parents to explain why their child is underweight, rather than to open up space for their perspective to be given.

2 Externalising

Within the narrative approach the person is never the problem, the problem is the problem. This belief challenges the assumptions that lie behind commonly used expressions such as 'problem child' or 'multi-problem family'. The narrative approach suggests that by locating the problem within the person, it is implied that the problem is a part of who they are. Talking about the problem in this way reinforces pessimism about the possibility of change, since it implies that fundamental changes in the person's identity would be required to remove the problem.

Externalising the problem means that the problem is something external to the person. Change will seem more possible if the problem is not intrinsic to the person. Externalising starts with the way the family describe the problem.

> Sam recounts the way his family reacted to his brother's suicide last year. He says, 'We were just overwhelmed with grief. Everything stopped at that moment.'
> The family worker responds, 'Can you tell me more about the ways grief has taken hold of your family?'

It's not up to the worker to try to convince the family that they ought to talk in a particular way. If they don't hear the family start to use the externalised expression themselves, the worker will need to try something else. Sometimes it's possible to develop a sense that the problem is separate, without finding a distinct name for it. Just the idea that 'it' or 'the problem' is pushing the family around may be enough to open up the conversation. Sometimes the worker may ask a family member how they would describe this thing that is bossing them around.

Externalising happens at different levels for different ages. While children often relate to 'monsters', teenagers may more likely respond to an externalised concept that involves an active rebellion, for example, 'kicking habits out of my life'. Adults may describe an externalised problem with a great deal of subtlety and nuances of expression. For example, a woman may experiment with describing a problem as 'being shadowed by fear' or as 'being harassed by fear' before deciding that the term 'being ambushed by fear' makes the most sense of her experience. Adults may be encouraged to try out new expressions that are free of the associations that permeate much of the language often used in discussions of problems. For example, 'guilt' may be described as 'self-blame'. Externalising creates the possibility of speaking to and of the problem. If the problem has its own identity it also has its own way of operating.

> Kathryn talks about how she is unable to stand up to her ten-year-old child because of the guilt she feels about leaving the child's father. Instead of talking about what it is like to feel that sort of guilt, the worker talks about the tactics that guilt uses. She asks Kathryn, 'How does guilt affect your better judgement?' Kathryn starts to make some discoveries about how guilt distracts her from the immediate issue. This opens up ways of tackling the problem.

One powerful effect of externalising is to reduce the extent to which an individual or family feel blamed or judged because of the problem's influence. Concerns are sometimes expressed that this may result in people's avoiding taking responsibility for what they are doing. However, workers using narrative ideas report that externalising the problem may in fact increase people's readiness to take responsibility. Because they now experience the problem as separate from themselves, they feel a greater sense of choice. While others may have told them they had to accept their responsibilities, they may not have experienced events as within their control. Rather than feeling paralysed by their inability to take charge, they may now see a choice between taking control of the problem and being controlled by it. Acting to take control becomes the ultimate evidence that externalising has invited them to take responsibility.

3 Unique outcomes

As well as revealing the strategies the problem uses to take control, externalising also opens up discussions about the way in which people have been able to escape being completely in the problem's grasp. Such instances are described as 'unique outcomes' or, more poetically, 'sparkling moments'. Often the impact of the problem has been so pervasive that instances when they have overcome the problem's influence have not even been noticed by the family, let alone accorded any significance.

> Rita has described herself as being 'stalked by self-doubt'. She mentions in passing that she had for the first time attended a meeting at her child's school. This was the kind of gathering that previously she had said she was unable to attend, because of the impact of self-doubt in her life. The worker drew attention to her attendance at the meeting and then asked questions about how she was able to escape the influence of self-doubt long enough to undertake this task and the sorts of strategies she used to keep self-doubt at a distance.

Sometimes unique outcomes may be hard to find. The family's story may seem so problem-saturated that workers will need to be particularly persistent. It is at this point that the workers' beliefs about the family will be far more significant than their experience with techniques. The worker who persists in looking for unique outcomes in the belief that each family brings their own particular capacities and knowledge of their situation will be far more likely to find 'sparkling moments' than the worker who is not working within this optimistic framework. When workers themselves are overwhelmed by the weight of the problem, pessimism can take over. Under the influence of this pessimism, the worker may get caught up with the use of labels such as 'resistant' or 'hopeless', and they may not be open to unique outcomes that challenge these labels. Another way of finding unique outcomes involves listening for what is not said in the family's story.

> The Hong family describes the way that 'temper' got the better of a child at bedtime during the week. The family worker checks how many nights were involved. A family member remembers that on Tuesday night 'temper' had not been evident. The worker starts asking questions about how the child was able to keep the temper at bay on such occasions.

If it seems hard to find evidence of unique outcomes in the present, another approach may be to ask about the past. For example, 'Is the temper as obvious during the holidays as it is in school time?'

For a unique outcome to become part of the development of a preferred story, it needs to be significant not just to the worker, but meaningful to the family and representative of something that they want to have more of in their life. This means asking the family questions such as: 'Would you like to have more of these experiences?'

It is important to check that what seems to be a 'sparkling moment' does have that meaning for the family. This process can be complicated when a family member seems to minimise the significance of the 'sparkling moment' almost as soon as it appears. When this happens it may be helpful to establish whether this is the dominant story reasserting its influence, or whether the action or event was so at odds with beliefs that are important to the person that it does not constitute a preferred experience.

> Roger has been working with Paul, a family worker, on ways to win back his life from the influence of self-doubt. He tells Paul about a situation in which he stood up to a teacher who had ridiculed his ten-year-old son, who has a learning difficulty. Roger ends his account by saying, 'Of course, I wouldn't ever want to do that again.' Paul asks whether self-doubt is fighting back. Roger replies, 'Maybe a bit, but I wouldn't want to have to rely on a shouting

match with someone to make my point.' This helps Paul to understand better how Roger would prefer to have his relationships with school staff.

A unique outcome is like a thread. Many threads will be needed to weave something new and substantial. This process can be referred to as 'thickening' the preferred story. The identification and discussion of unique outcomes provides alternative language for describing feelings and events, and different ways of understanding their significance. From these discussions can emerge a growing hopefulness that the person can be an agent in overcoming the problem, instead of being overcome by it.

Initially the language used to describe the preferred story may rely on externalisation. Sometimes further on in work with families there may be an opportunity to explicitly name the emerging narrative so that the family are in support of something, rather than continuing to use language that emphasises opposition.

> Margaret has been challenging the influence of self-doubt in her life. She describes what it was like to be asked to assist in a group at her local church: 'I actually felt like I was worth something!' The worker asks questions about what Margaret has found works for self-worth, as opposed to self-doubt. Further conversations focus more on the influence of self-worth, rather than the challenge to self-doubt.

4 Constructing preferred stories through questions

Asking questions is a familiar activity for family workers. Within the narrative approach, questions are used in a particular way. As unique outcomes are identified, the process of questioning is used to construct a preferred account of the family members' experience. The focus of questions is not on collecting information about the family or the problem, nor are questions used to encourage the family to come to a conclusion that the worker has already reached about them or their experience. Instead, through asking questions, the preferred story is constructed. The expression 'constructed' is used deliberately. The emphasis of the narrative approach is on creating alternative versions of the family's life, not on uncovering something that existed but had been hidden from view. The preferred story results from the unique collaboration of family members and family worker. There is no one 'correct' account.

'Story development' questions take those aspects of people's lives that have been less visible because of the influence of the 'problem' and set them in a new context (Freedman and Combs 1996, p. 131). They involve attention to details such as the steps a person has taken towards a preferred outcome, the reactions of others and the connections that can now be drawn between the present and the past, or the present and the future. These questions invite people to see themselves as active in their lives and to explore how they have taken this position.

> Fabio, a young man aged fifteen, is challenging the influence of 'trouble' in his life. He recently moved in with his father after being homeless for several months. He describes to the family worker an incident where he was annoyed by the behaviour of his younger brother, but was able to avoid getting into a fight.
>
> Some of the questions the family worker uses to develop the story include:
>
> - What steps did you take to ambush trouble when it ran up behind you?
> - Can you think of another time when you were able to get in before trouble had a chance?
> - How were the steps you took to put trouble in its place different from what you might have done when trouble was on top?
> - If your father had been there to see you at that moment, what would he have noticed?
> - Where do you see these new steps taking you?

'Meaning questions' invite people to reflect on how they make sense of events or experiences (Freedman and Combs 1996, p. 136). These questions might be phrased in terms of people's identity, learning or relationships, and so they create connections that 'thicken' the emerging story.

The family worker uses some of these questions to explore meaning with Fabio:

- What does it tell you about yourself that you were able to persist even though trouble was 'playing dirty' at the time?
- What does it say about you and your dad that you were able to hang in together, even though trouble tried to get between you?
- What advice would you give other young people who also want to put trouble behind them?
- What have you learnt from this that you could practise in the future to continue to put trouble in its place?

There is no formula for asking questions. Questions that externalise the problem, identify unique outcomes, inquire about preferences, develop the story and highlight meaning are all important. Workers would generally intermingle different kinds of questions, rather than asking a number from the same category. As practitioners become more confident, they are less conscious of the kind of question they are asking and more concerned about how the question can extend the process of constructing a preferred account of experience.

5 Finding audiences for the preferred story

The preferred story is sometimes described as something that needs not just to be told, but to be performed. For different families there may be many people who can see and appreciate the development of the preferred story and its impact on the family. They can become an audience.

Where family workers are part of a team, different members of the team who may have come to know the family may be a readily available audience. Some agencies have regular meetings between statutory workers and the family that provide different kinds of audiences and a natural opportunity for highlighting change. Workers need to be alert to potential audiences.

> Wanda, a family worker, was asked to prepare a report to support a claim for compensation following a car accident in which Violet, a passenger, was badly injured. In the report Wanda detailed the impact of the accident, but in the last paragraph she documented Violet's achievements in challenging the impact of the accident on her life. This served to support the application for compensation, to which Violet was entitled, and located a new audience for Violet's achievement, helping to ensure that she did not remain a victim for life.

Similarly some workers have assisted family members to assemble a 'support team' for their endeavours. The notion of a support team can be very meaningful, particularly if the 'problem' is described as having a range of forces working on its side. While some members of the team may be people in the family members' lives, such as friends, workers and family who are actually available to provide hands-on support and to be a day-to-day audience for change, other members may have a more symbolic role.

Pauline is developing a new story that highlights her competence as a sole parent. She has a noticeboard in her kitchen with pictures of her support team. One picture is of her aunt, who never let what others said stop her from doing what she wanted. Another picture is of her elderly neighbour who obviously enjoys Pauline's company. The third picture on the board is Diana, Princess of Wales. Pauline describes Diana as someone who tried not to let anything get in the way of her relationship with her children.

In some instances more formal opportunities exist for the performance of the preferred story. Gains made by the family can be recognised and celebrated with the presentation of cards or certificates and graduation ceremonies. Such activities can involve a range of people in the audience, including extended family and friends as well as workers.

NARRATIVE WORK IN CHILD PROTECTION

Narrative work emphasises respect in relationships with all family members and counters practices that families experience as blaming and judgemental. This aspect of the narrative approach raises challenges given the involvement of family workers in child protection. Family workers have responsibilities to make judgements about the safety of children. Workers can find themselves in conflict with family members over these judgements. This would suggest there can be a fundamental conflict between the narrative approach and child protection work. However, family workers using narrative ideas in child protection report that, rather than creating conflict, they find themselves able to openly address child protection concerns more effectively.

While the notion of blame is absent from narrative work, this does not mean that workers take a neutral stance. Working from the position that children should be able to live in a safe environment, 'safety' becomes, in a sense, a party in all conversations. This is made clear to families from the beginning of their involvement with the worker, as is the case in most family work settings. As a result, conversations around safety are possible that may not occur as readily in other settings that emphasise the worker's expert role in determining what is safe.

Sometimes naming the problem 'abuse' or 'violence' invites the recruitment of families to work for safety quite explicitly. For other families the language can be less explicit, but the use of externalisation enables workers to discuss the impact of the problem on the family without family members becoming sidetracked by questions of blame or fault.

> Julie and Matt had been very defensive in the past when asked how the bruises on their child's body were caused. A more open discussion occurred when the worker asked: 'Are there times when stress leads you to be doing things that you would rather not be doing?'

While developing a preferred story, workers acknowledge that the story needs to take account not only of the parents' experience, but also that of the child or children. From the beginning the range of questions should include the child's or children's experience. Some workers report that they find themselves more able to confront family members in this context, and that their work is more able to be explicit in drawing links between the adults' experiences and the meaning of those for their children.

> Julie described her experience of depression. The worker then asked, 'What part does your fight with depression play in your child's life?'

In situations where the family experiences a series of practical challenges, such as financial pressures, housing problems or illness, workers may find ways of linking these incidents meaningfully to the work of developing a preferred story. In the light of an emerging story even substantial crises, such as the placement of a child in care, may add new threads and the family may be able to persist with a sense of hopefulness.

> A temporary placement was arranged for Julie and Matt's daughter. Julie and Matt were very sad this happened but saw it as providing a necessary break for them to work out new strategies to overcome the hold that abuse has on their family.

Family workers using narrative ideas in child protection acknowledge that in some situations they will become aware that safety is being compromised to such an extent that statutory authorities will need to remove a child against the wishes of and without any co-operation from the family. An optimistic belief that the person is not the problem and the awareness of occasional 'sparkling moments' may not be a strong enough base to actively work towards the child remaining in the family's care at that time. Such situations can prompt a struggle to maintain optimism and raise questions as to whether parents do want to do the good things for their children. In such instances the worker using a narrative approach can enlist an understanding of the force of dominant stories that has an impact on parental behaviour. This understanding can assist workers to continue to engage collaboratively and respectfully with families while actively ensuring the safety of children.

> Carmel has been working with the Wilson family for the last six months. During that time she has seen clear evidence that the children are mistreated by their parents. This mistreatment has included locking the children outside of the house, tying them up and not providing adequate food. While the parents have attempted to change their behaviour, Carmel now believes their attempts are not enough to ensure that the children will be safe from physical and emotional harm. Carmel reminds herself of the childhood experiences of the Wilson parents, both of whom grew up in state institutions and received the message from the wider community that they were scum who would never amount to anything. When the Wilson's berate her for reporting the risk to the children, Carmel acknowledges their distress and affirms their determination not to abandon their children to the care of the state.

NARRATIVE APPROACHES TO DOMESTIC VIOLENCE

Contemporary approaches have involved challenging previously accepted views of domestic violence. Discredited, these views legitimated or excused violence by men towards women as 'provoked' by women or in other ways the fault of women. Narrative work has therefore fitted well for workers who had already gone a long way towards deconstructing dominant stories about violence. Narrative approaches offer a way of working with women that locates their experience within the wider social context and identifies the practices and beliefs in the community that support and legitimate violence. It encourages consideration of what it could mean to women to move beyond the influence of violence, both for themselves and their children.

Workers have found that as they have examined the pervasiveness of dominant stories about domestic violence, they have reached a better understanding of the factors existing in the community that perpetuate violence. This makes it easier to appreciate why it is so difficult for women to leave relationships where violence is present and why they return to those relationships. Such awareness provides workers with more strength to persist in spite of the influence of violence and invites workers to maintain a respectful attitude to women who still struggle against that influence. Involving women in conversations about the ways in which violence may persist in its attempts to influence their lives allows workers to talk about situations where women have re-entered a life under the influence of violence without their discussion becoming immersed in themes of blame and self-recrimination.

There is a common belief among those working with women experiencing domestic violence that women face little prospect of a violence-free lifestyle if they do not leave the partner who has been the perpetrator of the violence. This has extended to a view that, even with skilled intervention or access to legal processes, few if any perpetrators of violence will develop a commitment to a violence-free lifestyle.

Such beliefs may well be seen as yet another dominant story. This story replaces the earlier dominant story that women were responsible for domestic violence, but it continues to constrict the options for people to make sense of their experience and to find strategies for change. It can be argued that this new dominant story says that no man who perpetrates violence is able to change and that relationships in which violence occurs are totally destructive. This story continues the preoccupation with blame and guilt. Interestingly enough, with this dominant story women do not escape the blame and guilt—it is now focused on why women do not leave violent situations.

A narrative approach provides a way of opening the options and strategies available to women. It is an approach that acknowledges the impact of violence and the social context of the violence while focusing on the experiences of individuals and the meaning they bring to their relationships and actions. The worker listens for the meaning given by the family. 'Unique outcomes' where violence did not follow usual patterns can be explored openly. However, as in child protection, the worker using a narrative approach is not neutral about the issue of safety and will introduce the notion of 'safety' to all these conversations. This process can work toward the building of an alternative story for the woman, who may come to see herself not as a powerless victim who is totally controlled by violence, but as someone who is developing her awareness of her options and the ability to exercise them.

Within narrative work there is a concern that externalising violence, at least in conversations with family members affected by its influence, is unwise or even dangerous. The concern is that externalising may be seen by perpetrators of violence as another invitation to give away responsibility and may become another means by which violence is legitimated. One way taken by some workers to address this concern is to make a clear overt statement that people are responsible for their own actions, prior to externalising violence in discussions with the family.

Some workers using the narrative approach are challenging practices that seek to minimise any interaction between family workers and perpetrators of violence. They suggest that to work from the position that nothing positive can ever come from contact with perpetrators of violence can be seen as contributing to a new dominant story that supports the pervasiveness of violence because of its message that nothing can challenge or change violence. Such a story may allow more room for violence to take over the lives of families. These workers are developing new practices of including men in conversations with their families and providing programs that invite men to demonstrate a commitment to a non-violent lifestyle. Such practices reinforce the idea that perpetrators of violence are responsible for their actions.

NARRATIVE WORK AND POVERTY

Families who do not participate in the paid workforce may experience not only financial difficulties, but also conflict in relationships, isolation, mental health problems and challenges in parenting. The narrative approach challenges practices that see the personal difficulties experienced by families as independent from their social, economic and cultural context. Such practices may support explanations that view family members as individually at fault or personally deviant, with the use of expressions such as 'dole bludgers' or 'feral'. Alternatively, such practices may offer intervention for personal 'problems', such as depression or inadequate parenting, based on the assumption that these difficulties are solely a reflection of internal problems that can be addressed without reference to the family's context.

Narrative ideas have led individual workers to challenge their personal assumptions and to listen more actively for accounts of how families survive in spite of forces that are outside their control. This naming and challenging of dominant stories may occur both with individual families and in group work. As well as having an impact on work with people who are marginalised economically, narrative ideas have been used to bring together other groups, such as people affected by mental health issues and people from marginalised cultural groups.

> A group for lone mothers met at a family support service. They identified society's dominant stories about sole parenthood, such as women 'doing it for the money' and not looking after the needs of children. As a group they developed a preferred account of their lives that emphasised the strength it takes to parent alone and the support they could draw from each other in undertaking this task. Members of this group now look at resource material with a critical eye and a view to what fits their own experience and knowledge, rather than replacing their local knowledge with that of experts.

CHALLENGES FOR WORKERS USING NARRATIVE IDEAS

Developing stories that persist

The more threads there are to the emerging story, the more likely it is to persist in the family's day-to-day life. Keeping sight of the story can be challenging when families are in crisis, and it feels as though things are changing every day. Because family workers are involved in the provision of practical services as well as talking about the family's situation, it is not surprising that the threads of an emerging story can get lost in discussion of day-to-day matters. In addition, working in the family's home can involve coping with distractions that impact on the flow of conversations.

Workers report that with experience it becomes less difficult to draw new events into the language of the emerging story. Practice also gives workers more confidence to persist with asking questions and drawing out detail to create more layers to the story. While in the initial stages there may be concrete things that need to be done, such as locating financial or legal help, once a story starts to emerge, crises can be seen as hiccups, rather than evidence that good work has been undone.

One strategy to support persistence is for the worker to put the new story in writing. Family workers often find it hard to make the time to write letters but, as one worker puts it, 'a letter lasts'. One young person who received a letter from a worker documenting his achievements in 'pushing trouble aside' rang her to say he had never received a letter before, so that receiving this one created another 'sparkling moment'. Other documents such as court reports can provide an opportunity to write down the emerging story so that the family can refer to it. Certificates spelling out the achievements of family members are also valuable.

Working collaboratively

The narrative approach requires workers to put aside their role as experts in the lives of others. Workers may have to leave behind habits of relating such as offering interpretations of behaviour or diagnoses. When workers have developed expertise over years it can be hard to hold back from demonstrating it.

A different challenge for family workers may be leaving behind habits of supporting and presuming they know what is best for people. One family worker candidly describes this as 'giving up nurturing the problem for families'! Because workers who are paid and recognised for doing a job will always have a degree of power and legitimacy with that role, the process of questioning the impact of that power needs to be ongoing. One indication that workers are questioning their role is the expression of concern, rather than gratification, when people say, 'I couldn't have done it without you'. Another is hearing workers value the knowledge they have gained from families.

Confidence to be yourself as a worker

While the narrative approach has been extensively documented, it is much easier to grasp through direct contact with someone experienced with the ideas, or through watching the approach being used. While workers may find the cost of training limits their access to learning in formal settings, working jointly with a family with someone else who has had more experience with narrative ideas or even just talking to them about your work is likely to be worthwhile.

Because the narrative approach pays so much attention to language, workers sometimes feel that they need to sound like those who developed the narrative approach, in particular Michael White and David Epston (1990). Workers can run the risk of paying more attention to 'sounding narrative' than to the family's experience and so lose the family in the process. As one worker put it, 'I'd ask a "Michael White" question, and the family would just look at me'. As White and Epston would be the first to point out, everyone needs to do their own work. As workers feel more confident about doing what is appropriate for them and the family, they will get more done, and find more opportunities for their work to be creative and even fun.

Recognising the cultural context of stories

Sensitivity to the meaning located in the family's cultural heritage can add further threads to the emerging story. For this to occur, the worker needs to be listening carefully to the language the family uses and to the specific meaning cultural practices have for family members. This requires the family worker to put aside their own sense of the meaning of these practices, and to listen with respect for the meaning that fits for the family. In some situations, aspects of culture may be experienced as part of the dominant story that has oppressed the family. This is likely to be the case for family members where culturally prescribed beliefs about gender or status have supported the dominant story.

Alternatively, family members may experience their culture as supporting the emergence of a preferred story. This can especially be the case where families have experienced their own culture as devalued in the past. The development of the preferred story may parallel an emerging awareness of the significance of the family's culture. Culture can then become an additional resource for the family to draw on as the preferred story is developed. Culture that has different meaning for different family members presents particular challenges.

If workers seek a particular meaning to ascribe to cultural practices, they run the risk of limiting the family's story by stereotyping the family's experience, thus reducing the story's richness. Because workers are accustomed to feeling confident about their own views, it can be extremely difficult for them to put those views aside.

LIFE'S GOING AHEAD: DAVE'S STORY

Dave is a father and a step-father who lives with his wife in a coastal town. He attended a group run by the local child and parent support service because, as he says, 'being a step parent can be pretty hard'.

Dave's story highlights:

- the emergence of a preferred story about parenting, independent of his own experience of being parented
- the recognition of the 'local knowledge' of other group participants
- the role of group members as an audience for change.

I'd been married before, and had one child. Then I remarried, and we had the baby, and four step-children. One of the boys has special needs, and it was a lot to handle. My wife rang the service and they put us on the waiting list. I got on to them and explained what was happening and they sent a counsellor out. They told me they were running a group called 'Dads Can Do It Too' and I decided to go.

There were six men, different shapes, different lives. Some were in first marriages, some had been married before. The biggest thing was hearing the other blokes' stories. We'd hang out for Tuesday night when the group was on.

One session early on we all had to choose a picture. I chose the picture of a prison with bars. I felt like I had a weight round my neck. I was working three casual jobs. I was tired out and jumping down the boys' throats all the time. I'd come in after work and see things that hadn't been done and go off the deep end. I felt angry and it wasn't until I heard other men's stories that I found out I wasn't the only one dealing with this.

I found out that while I thought I was doing the right thing with the kids, really I wasn't doing it well. I started to realise that what your parents did changes you. You do what your parents taught you. I thought of my father as a loving man, but he was strict in his own way. The way he brought me up was 'do it or else'. I'd gone from being the father of one in my first marriage to the father of one plus four step-children and a baby, and my father's learnings clicked in.

On your own you feel like 'What's the point?' but in the group you know you're not alone. Being in the group made it easier to admit things and to realise I wasn't approaching things the right way. Someone would bring up a situation and everyone would throw in their ideas. The information just flowed. I'd bring home the notes and talk to my wife about it. We'd try different things. Not everything works all the time but that's okay. I now know I don't have to do it the way my father did.

One of the biggest changes was learning how to listen. I'd always been in such a hurry. Now I take time to listen to the boys. That opened up a whole new barrel of monkeys. I try to spend as much time with them as I can, and now the boys ask to be with me a lot more. I'll say I'm just going out to do something and they'll want to come to.

Rex, the group leader, was there to help but not to give you answers. I'd had counselling before with my first marriage and the counsellor used to say, 'I hear you say . . .' I hated it. Some of the other guys knew what that was like and we said to Rex, 'Just don't ever say that' and he never did.

Towards the end of the group we chose pictures again. I chose a brook with running water, because I felt more at ease, and a train, because now it's like I'm with the family on a trip and life's going ahead.

FINDING OUT MORE

Language is central to the narrative concern about the creation of meaning and becoming familiar with the style of Michael White and others who write about narrative ways of working takes time. Michael White has argued that the descriptions used in his writing should not be seen as obtuse jargon, but rather as 'precise meanings that the regular and taken-for-granted terms of the culture of counselling . . . cannot convey' (White 1997, p. x). Because of the challenges presented by some narrative sources, it can be helpful to start with material that describes narrative work in practice, rather than beginning with more theoretical material.

Freedman, Jill, and Combs, Gene (1996) *Narrative Therapy: The Social Construction of Preferred Realities*, W.W. Norton, New York. This book provides a systematic and coherent account of narrative practice with a particular focus on the use of questions, illustrated with examples drawn from practice, and with an extensive bibliography including White and Epston's work.

Lane, Kerry (1998) 'Mad Fax Sunday', *Gecko: a Journal of Deconstruction and Narrative Ideas in Therapeutic Practice*, 1: 45–61. This article illustrates externalisation and narrative use of questions, as well as the use of support teams for workers and family members.

Stringer, Anne (1998) 'Museums Join Others Against Violence',

Gecko: A Journal of Deconstruction and Narrative Ideas in Therapeutic Practice, 2: 46–50. This article describes a family worker's experience of finding an audience for change in a family friend.

White, Cheryl, and Denborough, David, eds (1998) *Introducing Narrative Therapy: A Collection of Practice-based Writings*, Dulwich Centre Publications, Adelaide. These descriptions provide an accessible starting point for exploring narrative ideas.

five

Cognitive work with families

Imagine two children doing their homework. Struggling with their maths assignment, they start to talk to themselves as they go.

'This is so hard,' says George, 'I'll never get it done.'

'I'll start with one I know I can do,' says Nick.

'The teachers shouldn't give hard homework like this,' says George. 'They're so mean.'

'I'm getting there,' says Nick. 'I can do it.'

'It's hopeless,' says George, screwing the maths sheet into a ball and throwing it on to the floor. 'I'll never be able to do it.'

'Phew,' says Nick as he packs away his pencils and book. 'I'm glad that's done. Now I can go and play.'

George and Nick had quite different responses when they found themselves in a challenging situation. George's thoughts kept turning to his difficulties with the task. The more he concentrated on the problems, the harder the homework seemed to get. Nick focused on the possibilities and was able to persist.

The cognitive approach suggests that how people think about difficulties can contribute to making those difficulties worse. George's thoughts focused on the difficulty of the task in front of him, they made him feel defeated and he eventually gave up, while Nick was able to think in a way that helped him to reach his goal. Both boys could have had the same ability to do their homework but the outcome was different because of their ways of thinking. Central to the cognitive approach is the premise that if unhelpful ways of thinking can be identified and modified, changes in how people feel and what they do can occur.

One pattern of unhelpful thinking occurs when people's thoughts do not fit with the facts.

> Tammy loses her cool while dealing with her two-year-old son's tantrum at dinnertime. She screams at the child. She thinks, 'I'm a hopeless parent, I never do anything right'. In her distress she finds it increasingly difficult to respond to her child at all and shuts herself in her room, leaving the child sobbing outside. What has not occurred to her are the previous times during the week when she coped with her child's behaviour without shouting or the fact that they had just returned from a shopping trip that was enjoyable for both of them. She has made a generalisation that is not supported by the evidence.

Sometimes people have thoughts that cannot be tested factually, but are just not helpful.

> Tammy thinks after she has yelled at her son, 'My child is going to be a terrible teenager'. She feels overwhelmed at the thought, visualising the police knocking at her door. Tammy has no way of testing out the reality of that thought right now, and it is of no use to her as she tries to cope with her toddler.

Negative thoughts pass through everyone's mind at some time. These thoughts flash past automatically, so that people may be barely aware of them. Much of the time such 'rogue' thoughts, including ones that emphasise a sense of failure or hopelessness, pass without impact. However, a range of factors can increase an individual's vulnerability to systematically focusing attention on these thoughts and interpreting them in ways that contribute to escalating distress. Such factors may include genetic traits and a range of life experiences, including childhood trauma. Patterns of thinking can also be affected by illness, lack of sleep or environmental stresses, such as living with a violent partner or not having a stable place to live.

The cognitive approach was first developed as a response to depression. By identifying and addressing a person's negative view of themselves, their environment and their future, it proved possible to achieve positive changes in their mood. While negative thoughts are not seen as the cause of the depression, they are one aspect of depression where intervention is possible. Intervention may occur in conjunction with strategies to address other aspects of the person's condition, such as drug treatment or practical strategies to reduce stress.

Subsequently these ideas have been applied to a range of difficulties where distorted cognitions or thought patterns can be identified. One of these difficulties is anxiety, where an individual's thoughts become focused on the possibility of physical or psychological threat. Another is panic, where potentially manageable situations are misinterpreted as catastrophic. Cognitive approaches to substance abuse have also been developed. These assist individuals to identify and address thoughts associated with continued substance abuse, while also encouraging alternative responses to the problems of daily living.

Because the cognitive approach was originally developed by practitioners with a strong interest in research and ties to universities, it has been studied extensively and documented in very systematic ways that have shown its effectiveness in addressing specific, identifiable difficulties. As a result of this work, practitioners have gained greater confidence in focusing on ill-founded or unhelpful thinking, rather than giving priority to questions about where that thinking originated. This approach has contributed to a greater sense of optimism about the possibility of change in response to what were once seen as invariably long-term and disabling problems.

The cognitive approach originated in formal, structured therapy settings where the focus was on the treatment of specific psychological disorders. Family workers often work with families in their own homes, and may be involved in addressing a range of issues. Although their contact with families may have a more informal quality, with less structure than a textbook approach to cognitive work, family workers are reporting that the cognitive approach can be useful in their work. In fact, family workers may not be aware that some familiar concepts such as 'self-talk' strongly reflect cognitive thinking.

Family workers often see family members who face difficulties such as depression or anxiety. For a range of reasons, family members may be unwilling or unable to access services where staff use cognitive intervention in a more formal setting.

Alison is a sole parent living in a housing estate on the city outskirts. Public transport is limited and Alison has little access to child care for her two preschoolers. Although she acknowledges that she is constantly tired and that even small difficulties seem overwhelming, she sees no point in taking up a referral to the nearest health centre. She is, however, willing to participate in home visits from a local support service.

In the country town where Jessica lives there is a long waiting list for the outreach psychologist who visits once a month. Although Jessica is finding her anxieties about her children's safety are starting to get in the way of coping with daily life, her situation does not yet warrant her getting priority for treatment.

Familiarity with the cognitive framework opens up the option for family workers to focus on thoughts, not feelings, when concerns are raised by family members. Even when workers are not actively trying to elicit a person's thoughts, they may emerge clearly in the course of discussion. While acknowledging feelings is a vital part of joining with families, focusing on feelings may not always be the most helpful strategy. With an awareness of the ways in which addressing thoughts can lead to changes in how people feel, workers have another way of responding in situations where they are concerned that focusing on feelings could lead to a family member feeling more stuck.

In a support group for young parents, Mandy voices the thought that she should never let her child play at the park even under her supervision because he might be abducted. The group leader is concerned that opening up discussion about such fears may contribute to an escalation of anxiety for Mandy and other group members. Since many live in units, access to the park is an important outlet for children and their parents and the group leader is not aware of any evidence that it is dangerous for children to play there. Instead of focusing on Mandy's sense of anxiety and what might underlie it, she asks Mandy about the evidence for her belief. As the group discusses this question, the group leader can sense the feeling of relief for Mandy and others in the room as they determine that on the evidence it is safe to use the park.

CHANGING WAYS OF THINKING

The cognitive approach has fostered a more optimistic attitude to intervention with individuals coping with significant distress. It encourages workers to look at what they can do in the present, without feeling that family members must revisit the past before they can experience changes in how they feel or behave. It has a particular attraction for workers who find an educative role fits comfortably with their personal style.

1 Identifying automatic thoughts

Cognitive work starts by assisting people to articulate automatic thoughts. Even thoughts that are quite influential may be scarcely recognised by an individual, who may be much more conscious of feelings or interpretations.

> Tamoe walks into her home and is confronted by a pile of used plates and a heap of dirty washing. She is more aware of the sinking feeling in the pit of her stomach and a sense of resentment that no one is going to help her than she is of the thought, 'I can't do anything right'. In a discussion with her family worker, Tamoe talks about how fed-up she feels about the house. She says, 'Last night when I walked in the door I just felt like I wanted to cry.'
>
> To assist Tamoe to identify her thoughts, the worker asks, 'What was going through your mind right then?'
>
> Tamoe's reply is still quite vague: 'I suppose I must have thought the place was pretty disgusting.'
>
> The worker then asks, 'What words would you have used? What did you actually say to yourself?'
>
> Tamoe says, 'I think I said "What a mess, girl, you're hopeless. You can't do anything right."'

Because everyone has thoughts passing through their head all the time, the key is to find the thoughts that are present at the times the family member feels most distress. This might mean identifying what someone was thinking at a time when they felt distressed in the recent past, as in Tamoe's situation, or it may focus on the distress they feel right now. These are the thoughts that can be used most powerfully in work with the family. It is also useful to consider what has prompted the family member to seek help and how useful the thought is in addressing their concerns.

> Josie has a three-year-old son Harry and has just discovered she is pregnant. While she is telling her worker about her pregnancy, she starts to cry. She says, 'I don't know why I'm crying, I should be happy about this.'

> The worker acknowledges her distress, saying, 'You're feeling confused?'
> Josie nods.
> Then the worker asks, 'What are you thinking right now?'
> Josie replies, 'That I won't be able to cope with two children.'

Sometimes asking if the person has a visual image to complement the verbal thought can add clarity. Although cognitive work emphasises verbal strategies, these can be used in conjunction with other techniques, such as those employing visual imagery.

> Josie's worker asks, 'Do you have a picture in your mind?'
> Josie says, 'One just flashed past of Harry running under a car while I was looking after the baby.'

Sometimes a family member may be concerned about several things at once. This can create confusion, as the conversation moves between concerns. Identifying which situation is of most concern can help focus the discussion.

> Josie has been distressed about other things as well as the pregnancy. She had an argument with her mother last night, and she is worried about Harry who is unsettled in child care. Rather than moving from one issue to another, the worker asks her to identify which situation has distressed her the most. She is able to recognise that although she has been upset about the other situations, her response to the pregnancy is the one that has caused her the most distress.

Automatic thoughts are the basic material of the cognitive approach. For some people, just making thoughts explicit is enough for them to recognise that they are not true or do not help.

> Josie has identified that she is thinking that she will not be able to keep her children safe once she has two children to care for. She is able to dismiss these thoughts saying, 'Listen to me panicking about closing the gate, when I won't even have the baby for another seven months.'

For other people, bringing the thought to attention does not prompt such an evaluation. The worker may then seek to identify thoughts that can usefully be addressed and evaluated, and to collaborate with the family member in this process.

2 Addressing automatic thoughts

Rather than attempting to convince the family member that a thought is irrational, the worker collaborates in a review of the evidence that supports the view that the thought is a rational or helpful one. While it may be tempting for the worker to jump in and nullify the thought by finding the evidence against it themselves, this is likely to leave the individual unconvinced. Actively involving the family member in the process also increases the likelihood that they will develop the ability to question themselves when the worker is not present. Questions that may be useful in this process include:

• What is the evidence for that?
• What would you say to a friend who voiced that thought?
• What other explanation could there be?
• What are the advantages and disadvantages of that position?

> When Tamoe articulates the thought that she is hopeless and never does anything right, the worker responds, 'All right, so let's check that out. Have you managed to do anything right today?'
> Tamoe says, 'I suppose I got here okay. And I did manage to hang out the washing beforehand.'
> The worker replies, 'So for today you have already done some things right. Has this been an unusual day?'
> Tamoe responds, 'I do a lot of things right, it's just every now and then things get on top of me.'

Tamoe has begun to generate an alternative response to invalid or unhelpful thoughts. She is starting to voice adaptive thoughts that can be substituted when she finds she is suggesting to herself that she is hopeless and can do nothing right. This is an opportunity for the worker to identify the adaptive thought and to highlight any changes in mood that are noticeable as Tamoe shifts her attention on to it. By routinely developing adaptive thoughts in response to automatic thoughts identified during sessions between the worker and family member, the skills in generating those thoughts can be practised.

> Rita describes a situation where she was running late to the doctor and started to panic. She comments, 'I actually started repeating to the kids, "We're never going to make it", which set us all off. I started to cry and I was dragging the kids along with them crying.

People started to look at us, which made me feel even worse.'

The worker asks, 'What was the worst thing that could have happened?'

Rita thinks about this and recognises that even though they were late, there was still lots of time for the receptionist to fit them in. She decides the worst thing that could have happened was annoying the receptionist.

The worker then asks, 'Can you think of something you could have said to yourself and the kids that would have fitted better with the circumstances?'

Rita suggests that another time she could say, 'We'll be there well before they close.'

3 Working with beliefs

As a worker assists a family member in identifying and addressing automatic thoughts, they may build up a picture of the beliefs that inform these thoughts. Beliefs have been described as 'relatively rigid, enduring cognitive structures which are not easily modified by experience' (Beck et al. 1993, p. 169). Rules or attitudes may work in a similar way. It has been suggested that at the root of all problematic beliefs are the themes that all is hopeless or that the individual is unlovable.

Identifying beliefs may not be easy, especially if the focus of sessions is diverted by recurring crises or the family are seen in their own home with the usual distractions. In such situations family workers may not be able to pursue the cognitive approach beyond the identification and review of specific thoughts as they emerge in discussion. This can still be useful, both in relieving distress and in assisting the family member to mobilise alternative, more helpful statements that can be used if the thought recurs.

However, where workers can develop some hunches about the kinds of beliefs that underlie the thoughts the family member has expressed, they can pursue these in more depth. Workers can develop a working model linking the thoughts that have been identified with an underlying core theme. This model is not seen as the truth about the person, but rather as a series of hypotheses that can be tested out as the work continues. The worker must avoid trying to convince the family member to accept their formulation of the belief. For useful work to occur, the family member needs to confirm that the belief identified fits for them.

> Bill and Marcia have been talking to a family worker for some time about the difficulties they have in dealing with the children. They have described patterns of behaviour where Bill withdraws from family discussions. Marcia is frustrated by Bill's lack of involvement in trying to discuss or deal with difficult behaviours. The worker has been asking questions about Bill's thoughts at these times and he identifies his thoughts as 'What's the point?', 'Nothing will change no matter how much you talk' and 'I don't think anything I say will help'. The worker wonders if underlying Bill's thoughts is a core belief that everything is hopeless. She starts to test this out by asking, 'Bill, do you have a sense that there is no hope that things will get better in your family?'

The process of dealing with beliefs is virtually the same as addressing automatic thoughts. It involves evaluating the belief by looking at the evidence that supports it. Then adaptive statements to counter the belief are developed.

Charting the process by which the belief developed is not essential to the cognitive approach. Some people may spontaneously start to draw connections between the belief and their experiences as a child or in later life. They may be able to identify people or events that contributed to the belief's development. Other people may not generate these ideas readily. Indicators that consideration of past events may be useful include:

- the family members start to make their own links with past events
- the work with the family has become stuck and the discussion of beliefs needs to be placed in context.

> Duong and her worker have identified 'I'm no good' as a core belief. One day Duong says, 'I want to tell you something I've been thinking about over the last week. I've never told anyone about this. There never seemed to be any point. When I was eight my uncle came to live with us. Over five years he used me sexually. He treated me like dirt. My life changed from that point. I was nothing.' Duong's collaboration in identifying a very influential belief provided her with a context for disclosing her experience of childhood sexual abuse.

As individuals are able to make significant changes in their lives, a ripple effect is often observed where change leads to more change.

4 Sharing ideas about change

An ultimate goal in cognitive work is to pass on to the family member the skills that will enable them to identify and address beliefs independent of the worker. Once acquired, these skills can be used throughout a person's life. If people see the process of change as a mystery, they may be inclined to credit the worker with the power to make change happen. If the process is made explicit, family members are more likely to take the credit for change themselves and to incorporate the steps into their approach to life, rather than attributing change primarily to the worker's intervention.

In addition to the identification and evaluation of thoughts and beliefs, cognitive work can incorporate teaching specific skills that complement the focus on adaptive thoughts and beliefs. Explicitly teaching problem-solving strategies and involvement in planning processes can be particularly useful.

Understanding how the cognitive approach works can also encourage greater optimism about the possibility of change. As family members develop an understanding of the links between thoughts, feelings and behaviour, they can recognise possibilities for modifying how they feel and what they do in situations where previously they felt everything was beyond their control.

> Over time Tamoe identifies a belief that life is beyond her control as the basis for her thoughts about her incompetence. She develops a range of positive statements as an expression of adaptive beliefs. There are still times when her home looks chaotic, but she is able to view this very differently. In her last sessions with the worker she could anticipate the worker's questions: 'I know what you're going to ask me,' she said, indicating that she has acquired an approach she can use independently.

5 Outside sessions: homework

Homework is an important aspect of the cognitive approach. Homework tasks commonly fall into three categories. These are:

- increasing activity
- practising noticing automatic thoughts and developing adaptive thoughts
- applying problem-solving strategies.

When people feel bad about themselves they tend to lose interest in activities that previously gave them satisfaction. This can become a vicious cycle where the less a person has to do, the more time there is available to dwell on the thoughts that are associated with feeling bad. Employing strategies to increase activity can intervene in the cycle. If an individual can recall an activity that they used to enjoy doing and is ready to try resuming it, at least in a small way, this could be presented as a homework task, with the details being developed in collaboration between the worker and family member. If the family member has difficulty recalling positive activities or feels unable to resume them, an alternative task could involve keeping a record of activity during the week and noting the associated feelings. This could enable the individual to identify which activities were more pleasurable. A further homework task could involve increasing participation in such activities.

The recording of automatic thoughts between sessions is a common assignment in cognitive work. Formats for recording thoughts and adaptive responses can be found in any cognitive text (for example, Beck 1995). They are useful tools for identifying situations that are triggers for specific thoughts, the feelings associated with them, options for adaptive responses and success in challenging beliefs. Such records can provide detailed information for discussion at subsequent sessions and can also reinforce ideas from previous conversations.

Barb is working with Stella. Stella felt overwhelmed by the responsibilities of parenting her three young children after her partner left.
Difficulties at work and with her family have also weighed on her.
During their first two sessions Barb and Stella evaluated some
automatic thoughts. Stella recalled that she was assigned a task
at work by her boss. She thought, 'I won't be able to get this done
in time'. She identified the feeling associated with this thought as
panic. Together with Barb she identified a useful response to the
thought by considering the questions:

- What was the evidence the thought was true?
- What would be the effect of believing the thought?

She developed the response, 'I've done this before. I can do it
again.' She then repeated the process with another automatic
thought. Barb suggested she keep a record of such thoughts at home.
Stella recorded what was happening when the thought occurred, the
thought and the feeling that was associated with it, useful responses

and the outcome. By the next session Stella recorded several thoughts and had found her evaluation of them helpful. When they discussed the record, some themes emerged in the kinds of thoughts Stella had recorded, which they evaluated in the session.

Some people will readily complete such tasks, while others may rarely do so. It can help if the worker has had experience in using the format themselves, even if they have little in common with the thought patterns of the family member. Individuals need to have practised the process with some positive outcome in the session before being asked to use it at home.

Acquiring problem-solving skills can be a valuable aspect of cognitive work. After using discussion of advantages and disadvantages as a problem-solving tool in a session, a family member may look for a situation to apply this to at home. This provides an opportunity for feedback, consolidation of achievements and discussion of difficulties when the worker and family member next meet.

COGNITIVE WORK AND CHILD PROTECTION

A cognitive approach to child protection can address specific factors that lead to harm or possible harm to children, and it can identify and address some of the consequences of those situations. Parents whose ability to care for their children is significantly affected by substance abuse or depression, for example, are unlikely to change their behaviour simply because they are directed to by protective services. In fact they will often believe such change is impossible. The provision of cognitive work for such significant difficulties will often be beyond the capacity of a family work service, necessitating referral to a specialist agency. However, an understanding of the cognitive approach can be valuable in several ways. Cognitive work is a popular treatment approach within such specialised agencies. An awareness of the cognitive assumptions about change can assist a worker to establish consistent messages and to positively reinforce situations where a family member is applying the model for themselves. A cognitive approach may also be useful at the referral stage in identifying and addressing thoughts that are associated with negative expectations of treatment.

Carla had been advised by the protective services that her use of alcohol was jeopardising her child's safety and court action was imminent. With her family worker she reviewed some of the pessimistic thoughts that had flashed past during her interview with the child protection officer and had contributed to her reluctance to pursue counselling with a specialist service. She was able to substitute the thought 'I've got nothing to lose—but my child', which was helpful as she underwent detox.

A common theme noted in work with children who have experienced abuse is the belief that they are responsible for what has happened to them. This can be one important factor contributing to a life-long sense of guilt and unworthiness, with far-reaching consequences. Cognitive work provides a theoretical framework for responding to such beliefs and may assist workers to address them more explicitly. Since many self-esteem programs are based explicitly or implicitly on cognitive assumptions, it is also useful for workers to have an understanding of how strategies such as creating positive self-statements or affirmations may have an impact (see Seligman et al. 1995).

COGNITIVE WORK AND DOMESTIC VIOLENCE

As the dynamics of domestic violence have been better understood over the last decade, it has been recognised that victims of domestic violence, both women and children, often believe that the violence of others in the household is their fault. This may be coupled with the thought that if they try, they can stop the violence by ceasing behaviour that triggers it.

While one strategy for addressing domestic violence is to emphasise that all family members have the right to live in an environment free of violence, this may not be meaningful for individuals who believe that violence is their fault. They may see discussion of rights as irrelevant, particularly if their cultural background does not emphasise personal freedom. Sometimes they may see the notion of rights as applying only to other people who, unlike them, are not at fault. Cognitive work suggests that an alternative strategy could involve focusing on thoughts and underlying beliefs about responsibility for violence. Rather than dismissing 'at fault' statements, the worker would engage in discussion about the evidence that the family member is to blame for the violence. Another area of work could be disputing statements which imply that a person should accept responsibility for changing the violent behaviour of another family member. The development of adaptive responses could then be undertaken.

Children growing up with violence are particularly vulnerable to experiencing life as beyond their control. At the same time their verbal skills may not be adequate to discuss their thoughts and beliefs in any depth. Cognitive strategies such as identifying and disputing beliefs about fault and blame may be supplemented by modelling adaptive statements, and using toys so children can rehearse new concepts at a distance.

> James was a quiet, withdrawn child, whose mother had recently left her partner after being hospitalised following a serious assault. While he was attending a group for children who had experienced domestic violence, James held back, but staff were conscious that he paid close attention to the contributions of other children. In a play activity James spontaneously took on the identity of the 'bad bear'. This provided an opportunity for the group worker to explore the world of the bear and in particular the evidence that he was 'bad'. Following this James became more active in the group, initially acting the part of a good bear using a puppet but then later referring to himself directly in some positive ways.

COGNITIVE WORK AND POVERTY

An individual's thoughts and beliefs are created and sustained in a context. While cognitive work may focus on cognitions, this does not mean that the family member's context can be ignored. In fact the more difficult the individual's life situation, the more time and care will be required to establish a trusting, collaborative relationship between the family member and worker.

A particular challenge is presented when a worker is confronted by the beliefs held by an individual who has experienced significant economic disadvantage. For a 40-year-old man who has not worked for ten years, the thought that he may never have a permanent job may seem to be an accurate, if depressing, evaluation of his circumstances. For a family facing the failure of a small business, the belief that they will be left with nothing to show for their efforts may seem impossible to challenge. Acknowledging these constraints can assist a worker to be realistic in identifying thoughts for evaluation and to be sensitive to the limitations of 'mind over matter'. At the same time, there is little doubt that the outlook of various individuals facing similar economic hardship can differ vastly. Finding out what adaptive statements assist individuals who seem better able to maintain an optimistic outlook could assist workers and families alike.

CHALLENGES FOR WORKERS USING THE COGNITIVE APPROACH

Engaging family members in a trusting relationship

In spite of its focus on rational interaction, the cognitive approach relies on the development of a sound alliance between the worker and family member. If the family member feels that they cannot trust the worker or the worker is dismissive of their difficulties, they will find it hard to be open about their thoughts and see little value in generating adaptive responses. While it is understandable that workers may become preoccupied with practising new techniques, they cannot substitute cognitive strategies for the work involved in engaging family members. This becomes even more important for families facing complex difficulties.

Adapting structured sessions to informal settings

The format of a structured cognitive session as described in the standard texts includes features that may be difficult to reproduce in family work settings where sessions are held at home or in response to crisis. These features include using questionnaires to check the family member's mood, collaborating to set an agenda and negotiating homework. Workers need to be realistic about their expectations of cognitive work in informal settings. They may well find that only a minority of families will end up taking on cognitive techniques independently. For others the main impact may be identifying some automatic thoughts and introducing the possibility of adaptive responses in specific circumstances in conjunction with addressing concrete concerns. In addition, if workers mainly see people facing very complex difficulties, they may not have the opportunity to practise cognitive interventions in straightforward situations where they can develop confidence and integrate their understanding of theory and technique.

Recognising the limits of the cognitive approach

Family workers often have contact with family members whose thoughts cause them considerable distress. While cognitive interventions have transformed the options available for people experiencing significant difficulties, such as depression and suicidal thoughts, they are in no way an instant solution. Workers need to recognise the limitations of their experience and the constraints of their services. Access to regular supervision and peer support can assist this process. Misplaced confidence in the application of cognitive strategies could have tragic results.

Disputing thoughts in context

A worker using the cognitive approach has a key role in challenging thoughts that are seen as irrational or unhelpful. For many people from a range of cultural backgrounds the notion of discussing feelings and options with a counsellor is unfamiliar. They may be more familiar with the notion of seeking advice or asking the opinion of someone wiser or better connected than themselves. This means family members may find it difficult to disagree with a family worker when it is suggested that a belief is unhelpful, even if they view their thoughts very differently. They may also find it difficult to understand how challenging their thoughts could make a difference to their situation, because their expectations of what will be helpful are vastly different. If their experiences of the concept of disputing beliefs are not helpful, they will not be able to generalise the skills and apply them to day-to-day situations.

Family workers using a cognitive approach need to be sensitive to the meaning of family members' beliefs in their cultural context. For example, many people would regard thoughts revolving around guilt or shame as unhelpful and would encourage people to dispute them. Many people would agree that young people need to think for themselves and develop identities separate from their families. However, depending on the cultural background of family members, such thoughts could have a very different meaning. The notion of independence from the family may be seen very negatively, perhaps as a sign of abandonment or rejection.

Inevitably workers will be influenced by their own values and experiences in assessing thoughts, and they must work hard to listen to the perspective of family members regarding the impact of specific thoughts. While this is always an important aspect of using a cognitive approach, it is particularly so if the worker comes from a different cultural background from family members.

I HAVEN'T LOOKED BACK: STEPHANIE'S STORY

Stephanie is a sole parent who lives with her children in an outer suburb of a large city. After leaving her husband she lived for some months in a women's refuge, where she had contact with a family worker.

Stephanie's story illustrates:

- the influence of beliefs on relationships
- the impact of identifying and challenging beliefs
- the ripple effect of developing adaptive beliefs.

> One day when my children were aged seven and five I came home to find my husband had gambled away the month's mortgage payment. That day I decided something had to change. I'd been making the decision to leave for seven years. I had gone before, but I'd gone back, and he'd left me at one point. I got an AVO [Apprehended Violence Order] while we were still together, which just made things worse. He thought I was trying to get our home, and he didn't give me any money after the AVO was issued. As well as gambling he drank. Our home was in a cul de sac, and on Friday night all the blokes in the street would head off together to one house and would drink till Sunday. Eighteen months after I left, the bank seized the house because the mortgage was in arrears. There was nothing left of my home.
>
> We'd been together for thirteen years. He'd only hit me three times but there was constant verbal and emotional abuse. He would come home looking for something I'd done wrong. One day he couldn't find anything, and he got out a white glove and ran his hand over the fridge top looking for grease. I look back now and think 'how crazy'. In the end I'd do stuff like leaving a basket of washing on the back step to get it over with when he first came home. I remember looking in the mirror and not recognising myself.
>
> I'd had depression on and off since I was eighteen years old. I'd had issues with bulimia when I was younger and with binge eating. I think I was vulnerable too from things that had happened when I was a teenager. I had allowed myself to be convinced that

I was no good. My father was a real perfectionist. If I got 98 per cent for an exam, he'd want to know what happened to the other 2 per cent. I didn't do well in my final exams at school, which made things hard with my parents.

After I left my husband I stayed in a refuge with the girls for six months and then moved into community housing. I had counselling and so did the girls. We had sessions together. I also went to a support group with other residents. I probably kept going longer than the others because I wanted to be really sure I could do it. I'd always been a giving person and a girlfriend said to me, 'Now it's your turn'. That really struck me because I'd never thought I was deserving of having things given to me.

In the groups we learned how to change our thinking. I remember we had to think of ten things that were good about ourselves. I couldn't find ten in the beginning! I learned that it was okay to treat myself, to have a bath and to relax. I learned to give myself positive messages. When I put myself down, the staff would challenge me about things I said that weren't true. I used to think I couldn't do things and I'd give a whole lot of excuses. Gradually I realised that I couldn't do everything, but I could do some things and the things I can do are my gifts.

Later the staff would ask me to explain to other residents how to motivate yourself. I remember learning to say to myself when it was hard to get started with the housework, 'I'll just do the bathroom'.

As a parent I expected myself to be perfect. But from when my daughter was four I couldn't work out what was wrong. I thought she had ADD [Attention Deficit Disorder], but not long after I left my husband I saw a psychologist who said it was my problem, it was the way I was bringing her up. That was the worst thing I could have heard, but I decided I wasn't going to change what I believed because of what they said. Finally I found someone to work with us who's brilliant. Now things are starting to turn around. I realise that I'm doing the best I can as a parent. If that's not good enough for someone else's standards then that's too bad.

After the refuge we moved into community housing on our own. The group I went to at the refuge really challenged the belief that women can't be whole without a man. I made a decision that my priority was the children, and we've been a complete unit, the three of us. I say to myself, 'It'll be over in ten years'. Since I learned to look at things differently, I haven't looked back.

FINDING OUT MORE

The cognitive approach has been extensively documented and systematically described in a range of manuals. These include considerations of cognitive work with various difficulties, including depression, anxiety and substance abuse. While these comprehensive publications do not address the specific challenges of family work, particularly in a home-based setting, they are valuable in setting out a detailed description of the approach. However, the impact of cognitive ideas has extended well beyond the clinical settings in which they were developed. For example, the cognitive approach has influenced a range of self-help books that practitioners may recommend to family members in conjunction with direct work.

Beck, Aaron, Wright, Fred, Newman, Cory, and Liese, Bruce (1993) *Cognitive Therapy of Substance Abuse*, Guilford Press, New York. This manual provides an extensive discussion of cognitive work with people affected by drug use and includes a discussion of management of life problems.

Beck, Judith (1995) *Cognitive Therapy: Basics and Beyond*, Guilford Press, New York. This book is a readable account of cognitive work with relevant guidance for beginners. Though not written specifically for the family work context, the ideas could be readily applied to family work settings.

Seligman, Martin (1990) *Learned Optimism*, Random House, Sydney. This popular self-help book includes information about cognitive interventions and addresses some of the wider applications of these ideas.

six

Community building and family work

Imagine three people who want to get fit. They have all decided to take some regular exercise. One buys an exercise bike and sets it up in front of the television. He plans to use it at least half an hour per day. The second person decides to take walks twice a day around her neighbourhood. The third person decides to take on the task of regularly walking the new family pet, an energetic puppy.

After three months, all three people have stuck to their exercise plans. The person who used the exercise bike is feeling fit. The people who walked around their neighbourhood are feeling fit too. But the people who walked also feel differently about their community.

The person who has been taking regular walks on her own has started to recognise some familiar faces. She is greeting more people at the local shops and on the bus on the way to work. She enjoys the feeling that she is a part of a community. The person who has been doing his exercise in the company of the puppy has made even stronger connections with his community. Lots of people, young and old, have stopped to talk with him and admire his pet. He now knows some of his neighbours' names. When one of his neighbours who has young children tells him of her concern about animal droppings in the local park, he goes to the local council to see if they will put a bin in the park for pet droppings.

Community building is concerned with developing connections between individuals to make communities better places in which to live. The community-building approach is strongly influenced by recent developments around the concept of 'social capital'. Social capital is a way of describing the glue that holds social structures together and is 'created from the myriad of everyday interactions between people' (Bullen with Onyx 1999, p. 3).

Elements involved in social capital include:

- networks that link people
- the degree of trust between people
- shared expectations about behaviour (norms)
- evidence of working for the benefit of the group (mutuality)
- doing things for others in an expectation that in the long term benefits will be returned (reciprocity).

Where there is a lot of social capital, people are more likely to feel they are part of a community. Families are more likely to be able to carry out their functions of supporting and nurturing their members. When families are fully embedded in their community they are more able to draw on important resources that are critical for their well-being. These include goods and services as well as less tangible resources such as emotional support. Conversely, in communities with low stocks of social capital, families are more likely to be vulnerable to isolation and less likely to be able to access resources. Family work targeting change in families must therefore take into account the community context in which a family lives.

Many family work programs have long histories of involvement in community development. The term 'community development' covers a broad range of ideas and activities about how to improve a place for the people living there. Some of these ideas have focused on infrastructure, both in terms of building and services. Activities such as needs analysis, planning, consultation and submission writing are undertaken in order to bring appropriate resources into the community. Another focus is on the distribution of power and control in decision making in communities. Community actions such as lobbying, media campaigns, public protests and boycotts are often a concrete part of this focus on power. However, activities solely addressing inadequate infrastructure or the unequal distribution of power assume that the people who live in an area can function as a community and are able to work together.

In recent years there has been a growing interest in what makes a group of people a community and how to build communities. Understanding social capital and how it is generated has extended thinking about how to improve community life for families. Interest in social capital has drawn attention to the need to have the basic foundations of networks, trust and self-worth in place. These are the prerequisites for participation in community life.

A focus on community building provides an avenue for validating a range of activities that family workers have long promoted. Approaches to family work that contribute to the development of social capital are not new. Isolation has long been recognised as a critical indicator of a wide range of family stresses and is linked to child abuse and other signs of the breakdown of the family unit as a place of nurture and care. Practice wisdom within family work recognises the value of programs such as playgroups for children and parents, parent support groups and family camps. However, family workers have lacked concrete ways of articulating how such activities with families can impact on communities. Researchers have seen changes within families as significant, but little attention has been paid to the details of the relationships families have outside the family unit (Webster-Stratton 1997).

The notion of social capital implies that some kinds of relationships do a lot more for individuals and families than others. Social capital will be enhanced by activities that promote trust, embrace diversity and increase social interaction. Family workers can add value to many of the strategies through which family work services are delivered. Although the tools for measuring and comparing social capital are still being developed, even quite simple measures can still be useful.

Family workers in Scott's Gap, a new housing area, conduct short-course parenting groups. They build into the program some ways of promoting links between group members, such as a long break for morning tea, a final lunch at the end of the course and the opportunity for group members to exchange phone numbers. When they evaluate the group they ask participants a range of questions. Some of the questions are about the impact of the group on their parenting style and on changes in children's behaviour. Others ask whether a parent has made phone or personal contact with another group member outside the group time. The workers are pleased to find out that 75 per cent of group members have increased their social network as a result of the group. They recognise that outcomes such as this are a vital building block for the creation of a community with reserves of social capital that families can draw on in times of stress and crisis.

The community-building approach assists family workers to recognise why it is valuable for families in vulnerable circumstances to participate in activities that build networks. However, the probability of people participating in such activities is much greater when potential participants are involved in their planning.

Shirley, a family worker, is close to finishing a twelve-week course for women affected by domestic violence. Participating in the group has been a very powerful and important experience for many of the women, and they have formed close bonds that Shirley is keen to encourage. In the final meeting, one of the women suggests they start a ten-pin bowling team. Shirley is concerned that a bowling alley may not be an appropriate venue to build on the strong emotional sharing the women have experienced in the group. She would like to encourage them to have regular coffee mornings in a quiet venue, perhaps with occasional guest speakers. However, Shirley recognises the interest shown by several of the women in the idea of bowling.

Two years later, many of the group are still going bowling together and play in regular competitions. They continue to provide each other with practical and emotional support.

The new understandings provided by the concept of social capital have been particularly significant for those working with families in vulnerable and isolated situations. Such understandings have explained why traditional strategies of community development have often been unsuccessful in the most disadvantaged communities where the need for change is most evident. The failure of residents in such communities to get involved in social action strategies may have seen them labelled as 'apathetic', 'anti-social' or 'lazy'. The community-building approach recognises the need to work on strategies that build links between people so trust and a sense of mutual concern and reciprocity can develop. Community development is based on trust and reciprocal relationships. Without these people cannot come together to work for change.

Karima is a community worker based in a family agency. When she first starts work she is full of ideas about how to make a difference in the very disadvantaged community in which the agency is located. She does surveys to find out local needs. She organises a public meeting for residents to discuss these issues. She plans the meeting carefully, with lots of publicity and a barbecue. Only a handful of people turn up, apparently for the free meal, but they don't contribute at the meeting. She then tries doorknocking, but people seem very suspicious. Nothing she does seems to interest the community. She feels very discouraged.

Karima then changes the focus of her work within the agency. She runs a number of courses on assertiveness and clear communication. After six months there is a regular coffee morning involving about fifteen residents who have attended the courses. Karima organises occasional guest speakers on topics ranging from first aid to craft activities. One morning the speaker is talking about the importance of play for children. The women at the coffee morning start discussing the lack of parks with play equipment. Karima suggests some ways in which some community action could take place on this issue. To her surprise, the women are very interested and start planning what to do.

Community building provides an alternative to a preoccupation with the needs and problems of communities. In fact the process of attracting funding for community resources is often based on cataloguing the community's deficits. While clearly resources need to be allocated with a consideration of need, this focus on the weaknesses of communities can become dispiriting for both workers and residents. Ironically, while highlighting problems may be effective in attracting resources, a focus on problems may not be the most effective starting point for those who want to enhance the community's potential.

In contrast, a community-building approach is optimistic. It encourages a focus on what is unique about the way the community operates, rather than emphasising what is missing in the community. Looking for assets such as reserves of social capital can provide valuable information about the resources of the community.

Jim opens the door with a sigh. He has seen Terry, a community worker armed with a clipboard, coming up his front path. He guesses that Terry will be just another outsider asking questions about the problems in his community. 'You'd think it would be obvious,' Jim thinks to himself, 'with all those young hooligans out on the street terrorising the neighbourhood and playing chicken in the traffic with their ballgames.' But when Jim starts talking to Terry he is surprised. Terry tells him that a new skateboard ramp is being planned and he wonders if Jim could help in any way with a sausage sizzle they are holding as a fundraiser to build it. Terry has a list of what could help, including the loan of a barbecue, an hour of time to cook sausages, distributing some leaflets about the barbecue in letterboxes or cutting up onions at the community hall the night before. Jim thinks a bit and then says that he can bring down his portable barbecue—as long as he is the only one who operates it! He also says he has a mate who delivers for a butcher who might be able to do a good deal for the meat.

BUILDING THE SOCIAL FABRIC OF A COMMUNITY

While stocks of social capital may be found right across a community, there appear to be some points in community life where there is great potential for community building. Families with young children are often described as being vulnerable because caring for children is a demanding task. At the same time there is great scope for families with young children to be involved in community building because children create links. These links can be both formal, through child care and other group activities, and informal, as the adults are drawn into relationships as well as the children. The reserves of social capital created at this time may prove significant in the life of the community for years to come.

Recognising points in the life cycle of individuals, families and communities where the potential for generating social capital is maximised can help workers to better understand why some community initiatives rapidly take on a life of their own, while others fail to gain momentum. This may also assist workers when they need to make difficult decisions about where to direct scarce time and resources.

1 Developing human capital—self-esteem and communication skills

Social capital requires human capital. Human capital is made up of the skills and knowledge held by individuals in a community. Without human capital it is not possible to undertake activities that generate social capital. Self-esteem and communication skills have been identified as two essential prerequisites for such activities (Bullen with Onyx 1999). Family workers are adept in using strategies to develop self-esteem and communication skills because they are the basic tools for families to use when identifying needs and working for change. The challenge of the community–building approach is to consider the context in which tasks that focus on aspects of communication and self-esteem are undertaken. If social capital is to be generated it is imperative that families have the opportunity to develop networks within their communities to use these skills. If these skills are taught and developed in isolation from the community it is less likely that they will be used to generate social capital.

Staff at a community-based family support agency have been running short-term courses for a number of years. They include 'Communication in Your Family', 'Standing up for Your Rights' and 'Building Your Confidence'. Over the years a large number of people have attended these groups and they have been valued highly by participants. However, there was little contact between most participants once they had finished their course. Recently, the agency has intentionally encouraged links between participants. Barbecues have been held at the conclusion of each group and participants have been encouraged to socialise informally and exchange contact details. Camps where groups of people go away for a weekend have led to the development of strong connections between families. Staff have been surprised by the camps' unexpected spin-off—the continuing links between families. There is now a much greater interest by families in contributing to agency activities. A small group have started to plan regular functions for all users of the agency. Another group have run a street stall to raise funds to organise another family camp. Two people are interested in being involved in the management committee of the agency.

Of course, there are many situations when initial contact with families will take place in isolation from community networks. Home visiting and other outreach services have been a cornerstone of family support services for over twenty years because they provide an effective way of delivering services to families who do not feel confident in accessing centre–based activities. A legitimate role for family support services is to provide avenues for families to access the service's network and resources. Individual counselling and home visiting can also be very important to the development of a trusting relationship, modelling one of the essential elements necessary for the development of social capital. However, it is imperative that longer term contact incorporates opportunities to build broader networks for families.

2 Increasing the material wellbeing of families

When people are struggling for survival, it is difficult for them to engage in activities that generate social capital. Their struggles lock them out of a process that would otherwise give them access to the resources provided by being part of a community network. This is part of a vicious cycle of poverty. This issue is more fully explored later in this chapter in the section on community building and poverty. Family workers operating in areas where there are low levels of social capital cannot ignore the financial needs of families.

> Staff at Greydome Family Services have initiated a range of activities to address the financial needs of the families in their area. Greydome has a large number of people who are unemployed or on other social security benefits. There is limited public housing. Many families face a continual struggle to pay for the basics of housing and food. A food co-operative operates from the family service, which provides fruit, vegetables and meat and a canned-food pantry is also on the premises. In return for packing the food people can obtain food at very low prices. Once a month there is an 'exchange market' at the service, where people can bring in items of clothing to exchange.
>
> The family workers have lobbied hard for government funds to buy goods and services as part of the action plan for individual families. These funds could be used for a wide variety of purposes: medical equipment and treatment, provision of child care, transport and holidays for families in need.

3 Developing physical infrastructure

Access to venues and activities that enable residents to develop relationships and to find others on whom they can rely is an important prerequisite to community building. Facilities such as local schools, parks and shops are not just a matter of convenience but necessary for the development of social capital. They provide the physical location where people can meet and interact. Individuals and families may survive without such opportunities, but the long-term impact on the reserves of social capital and the quality of life in the community is likely to be destructive. Many communities, particularly in rural areas, are feeling the impact of losing community services and meeting places that once were taken for granted. Bank closures, rationalisation of post offices and the loss of small shopping centres result in fewer opportunities to generate social capital.

Other aspects of the physical environment will also have a great impact on the creation of social capital enjoyed by families. Adequate transport links make it possible to sustain relationships and networks. Good lighting in public places will help residents feel safe in their neighbourhood. Good housing estate design can increase the opportunity for positive contact between families.

When the physical infrastructure is lacking, family workers have a role in identifying a community's needs and helping to lobby to remedy the situation. Such work can be time consuming and often requires the development of personal links with decision makers. In areas with low social capital, workers may need to take a more active leadership role in lobbying activities.

> People from Sunside had been working for eighteen months to get bus shelters installed along the main route to town. They had written letters and collected signatures for a petition without any impact. However, things changed when the staff from the local family centre asked the local member of parliament to accompany them and one of their families on a trip to town. It was a very hot day and the politician saw first hand the effect of the lack of shelter as the family went shopping. The family also told him what it was like when it was wet.

Sometimes it will not be possible to turn back the clock and replace facilities that used to exist in an area. This situation requires consideration of alternative ways of ensuring that community members can make connections and maintain networks and relationships. Innovative use of other community resources such as schools and health facilities can help and meeting places such as laundromats and transport interchanges can provide necessary physical infrastructure.

Physical amenities in themselves do not build communities. These amenities make possible activities that generate the building and sustaining of networks. Facilities that have been poorly planned or designed and have no relevance to local residents will not be used. When social capital is lacking in an area, a building will not make the difference. In these circumstances it is necessary to provide the human capital to initiate activities attached to the building.

> A new housing estate was established on the outskirts of a major city. In the centre of the estate was a community meeting hall,

which was prominently featured in the design of the estate. The prospectus talked about the hall as being the 'heart' of the community—a place to relax, meet friends and hold events such as birthday parties. All other facilities—shops, schools and sporting clubs—were located a distance from the estate. Within days of the estate opening, the meeting hall was the subject of vandalism. It was covered with graffiti. The lights around it were smashed. People avoided it and no one inquired about using it for family celebrations.

About a year after the estate opened, a community organisation from the next suburb considered setting up an outreach program in the estate. They were getting a huge number of referrals from families on the estate. They arranged to use the community hall five mornings a week. For the first three months they had a worker on site full time. She employed local high school students to clean up the graffiti and arranged for the lights to be repaired. She made a point of eating her lunch outside the hall whenever the weather permitted and chatted to people as they went past. Soon a program of regular activities was established, which included a playgroup, a craft group and regular visits from the early childhood nurse. There is still some occasional graffiti, but this is cleaned up regularly by the estate managers. Local residents are now using the hall and it is booked most weekends for family and community functions.

4 Promoting family-friendly practices

Family workers have a role in promoting community norms that are supportive of families. Sometimes this involves challenging assumptions and practices that make it difficult for families to participate in community life. Issues such as access for strollers to buildings and transport services, provision of child care or play spaces during public events and work practices that recognise the importance of parental responsibilities all involve examination of the norms of the community regarding the place of children and families. Family workers can contribute to changing community norms by raising such issues.

Staff at the local library are fed up with children left unattended during the evening. The children can be very disruptive and need a lot of supervision. The librarians see the parents of these children as irresponsible and have banned all unattended children. This comes to the attention of staff at the local family centre. They are concerned because they know some local single-parent families drop their kids at the library so they can do the shopping after work. The family centre staff know the parents who drop the children at the library do so to ensure quick and relatively stress-free shopping.

The family work staff speak to the library staff, and explain why the children are being left at the library. They discuss possibilities of alternative arrangements, such as evening play and craft sessions in the library at advertised times, negotiating with the shopping centre management for use of a vacant shop for children's activities and extension of a local church's children's club to include a 'Shopping Session'. The library staff agree to hold off the ban for several weeks while alternatives are investigated.

5 Providing opportunities for people to connect

Shared activities are the means by which social capital is generated. When the necessary prerequisites are in place—human capital, adequate levels of material wellbeing and physical infrastructure—it is possible for people to undertake such activities. In areas with low social capital it may be necessary for workers to organise such activities initially. However, participating in shared activities starts the process of building communities.

Workers in a community development project are aware of the low level of participation in community activities in Brushtown. Brushtown is a public housing development where unemployment is very high, transport links are extremely limited and there is a high level of juvenile crime. Brushtown has a bad name as a dangerous place to live and residents don't like to admit they live there.

The workers make contact with several families who have football-mad children. They play in school teams, but are not part of a weekend competition because transport to other grounds is difficult. The workers organise a bus and register a Brushtown team in the competition. Families of the children involved hold raffles for funds for the football team, and the local hotel supplies the uniforms. A growing network of families becomes involved, and the team attracts a loyal following who travel with them on the bus to the away games. They are proud to support the Brushtown team.

Natural disasters can reveal the existence of reserves of social capital in a community. In communities with high stocks of social capital it could be expected that residents would give priority to actions that would be of mutual benefit, and would look out for those who need assistance. Disasters might also be opportunities for the generation of social capital, where people are brought together for the first time, or where residents experience mutual reliance and trust.

A blocked stormwater drain creates a flood in an area serviced by Timberland Family Support Service. The service's own building is waterlogged, but the staff take the time to set up an information board outside their building listing the jobs that people in the affected area need assistance with. Many people speak afterwards of the unexpected outcomes of the flood. People worked together, neighbours got to know each other better and there were many examples of people caring for others. 'It really brought people together,' says one resident of a badly affected street. 'We are planning a street party next month to thank everyone who gave us a hand.'

6 Encouraging diversity

Social commentator Eva Cox has emphasised the importance of diverse social contacts in the creation of social capital. According to Cox, 'Family and intimate social relationships may limit our world views if they fail to offer us contact with strangers' (1995, p. 31). If social contact is confined to 'people like us', people are likely to experience their prejudices being reinforced and their anxieties confirmed. Where social networks develop across pre-existing groupings in society, the impact of trusting relationships will be greater. Inclusive practice is integral to the creation of social capital. Family workers report that prejudices and stereotypes can be powerfully challenged where the opportunity exists for interaction and exchange.

Two women meet at a group for women affected by domestic violence. They find they have lots in common, and provide support to each other as they seek to establish a life without violence for their children. For one of the women, it is the first time she has had a close friend from a different cultural background. Her own stereotypes about difference are powerfully challenged by the experience. This also has an impact on the messages she gives her children and the way she relates to parents from the diverse community at the local school.

Recognising the value for families of having a worker who speaks their language and understands their culture, family services often seek to recruit staff who are representative of the population they serve. Such practices can increase the interaction of people from different backgrounds across the service's programs and also mirror this diversity in the interaction of staff. Organisational values, policies and procedures can play a part in increasing social capital.

> Staff from Mildhill Family Services discuss the issue of reconcilia-
> tion between Aboriginal and non-Aboriginal Australians. They want
> to work towards reconciliation with Aboriginal families, but are not
> sure what is appropriate. They think of asking a representative of
> an Aboriginal organisation that provides services to families in their
> area to come to one of their staff meetings to talk about this.
> However, they finally decide that it would be more appropriate for
> them to go to the Aboriginal organisation, even though they feel
> uncertain and a bit uncomfortable about how they will be received.
> Their action in going outside of their own comfort zone is, in fact,
> greatly appreciated by the Aboriginal workers. The two organisa-
> tions develop a relationship of mutual support and share together
> in a reconciliation event that is attended by many families—Aborigi-
> nal and non-Aboriginal.

7 Using natural networkers

Although people often talk about 'the community' as though society consists of one integrated group, the reality of community life is much more complex. Multiple groupings within society can be iden-tified and they have complex webs of relationships. Groupings may exist around neighbourhoods, shopping centres, workplaces or key centres such as schools. Even referring to a particular 'ethnic com-munity' is often a gross simplification.

Social capital is a product of social interactions. Just as some activities provide opportunities for the generation of social capital, some individuals are particularly active in connecting different net-works. These 'natural networkers' may not hold formal office but they are a valuable resource nonetheless. Their knowledge of a wide range of people across networks enables them to bring together people with common concerns, whether these involve individual interests or broader political concerns.

> Myra is a member of a playgroup where she meets Jane, a parent
> of a young child with a disability. Myra also works at the school
> canteen, is involved in Girl Guides and is a member of a local

church. She invites Jane to her place for coffee and to meet Helene and Mac, other parents she knows who have experienced similar challenges with their own child.

Recognising and using the knowledge and skills of 'natural networkers' can enhance a range of activities for the benefit of families. Because of their connections they can effectively receive information 'on the grapevine'. They are the people to ask if someone with particular skills or experience is needed. They can be strategic people to inform about new services, or to provide with information about new ideas, because they interact with such a variety of people. It may even be that the skills of the networker can be modelled and learned by others, so that a wider range of people can develop their networking capacity.

8 Promoting connections with decision makers

Communities are strengthened through interactions of people through formal and informal associations. One aspect of social capital is the reserves of trust that exist between people and decision makers.

Decision makers, including politicians and people working within bureaucracies, are often viewed with distrust by individuals, particularly when those individuals perceive that they have little real influence over government activities. Government may be seen as remote and as favouring elites or cliques. At the same time, there exists within at least some arms of government a concern for greater responsiveness and a recognition of the need for more effective community consultation. Such is the prevailing pessimism about the ability of ordinary citizens to influence government processes that, even when opportunities for participation and feedback exist, people may lack sufficient trust to be involved.

Family workers can play a strategic role by bringing together decision makers and people whose life experience can provide information in a way that statistics alone cannot. Just to meet previously faceless bureaucrats or politicians can be an affirming experience for people who had assumed that their opinions were of no importance.

Parents from a playgroup operating in a local family support service discuss how difficult it is to cross the road to reach the centre. The family support worker organises a meeting for them with a manager from the government body responsible for road crossings. He listens to their suggestions and says that, while he can't promise anything, he will investigate the situation. Back at the playgroup, the parents tell others about the meeting in very positive terms, emphasising how the manager took written notes of their ideas.

Such contact may require workers to examine their own distrust of decision makers, and to be prepared to take some risks in the process. At the same time, the significance even of small interactions between government representatives and local people, particularly where such contacts have historically been rare, should not be overlooked.

Parents attending a support group meet a representative of the statutory child protection service. They discuss some of the challenges involved in ensuring children's safety. This makes a significant difference to how those parents perceive 'the welfare'.

As well as facilitating contact between families and decision makers, family workers often have opportunities to liaise with different tiers of government in relation to funding and coordination of services. Sometimes such interactions are described primarily as a rational process, where workers are able to share information and plan and coordinate services on the basis of a common understanding of needs. In practice, however, interagency activity often seems to be far from rational, and can be dominated by suspicion and rivalry. Pressures such as competitive tendering for scarce funds can make it even more difficult to maintain trusting relationships between agencies.

Thinking about interagency contact in the light of creating social capital can help explain why even quite superficial social contact between staff of different agencies can have an impact on working relationships by generating trust and expectations of mutual support. Equally important is the development of patterns of ongoing interaction if stocks of social capital are to be maintained over time.

Staff at a family centre arrange a lunch with the local child protection service. Relationships between the services have been rather strained, and it's a relief for staff just to chat socially. The next time a child protection officer makes a referral, they feel a bit more warmth over the phone from staff at the centre. The staff member allocated to work with the family feels more committed to keeping communication open. Over time relationships between staff at the two organisations improve, and families are benefiting. To ensure that newcomers to both agencies can play their part, the agencies organise social events about every six months.

COMMUNITY BUILDING AND CHILD PROTECTION

Recent developments in child protection have challenged the view that child abuse can be understood solely as a problem related to what happens within families. Isolation has long been recognised as a risk factor in child protection and is generally seen as evidence of the family's inadequacies regarding relationships. New research, however, has found that isolation is not just a reflection of the limitations of individual families, nor is it solely explained by the impact of poverty on a family's ability to make and maintain social connections (Vinson, Baldry and Hargreaves 1996).

Studies have compared rates of child protection concerns in neighbourhoods with similar socioeconomic conditions but different rates of social cohesion. Isolation appears to be significant not just because families are unable to access practical support from friends or more formal sources, but also because they are living outside the influence of socially determined norms about what is acceptable care of children. Garbarino and Kostelny have compared what they describe as high-risk and low-risk neighbourhoods and suggest that the attitudes of workers are also influenced by these dynamics. In the high-risk community, staff who were interviewed described a situation in which their agencies mirrored the isolation and depression of their community. In the low-risk community, the agencies mirrored the strong informal support network that existed among families in their community. They seemed hopeful because many of their families were hopeful (Garbarino and Kostelny 1994).

These findings suggest that stocks of social capital play an important protective role for children. While individual family issues are significant, the context in which the family lives may influence the development of norms around parenting, patterns of interaction between parents, children and other key people, and even the attitudes of professionals working with families. Strengthening communities does not just make them more pleasant places to live, it can also ensure children are safer.

The community-building approach promotes social interactions characterised by trust. Home visiting has been suggested as one strategy that engages families in such interactions. Interest has grown both in the value of professional home-visiting services and home visiting by volunteers. Home visiting by paid family workers can engage families on their own turf and provide links with a range of other agencies. Volunteer home visiting seeks to duplicate the kind of practical and emotional support that might otherwise be provided by family or friends, and enables the family to benefit from the formal and informal networks of the volunteer. Although home-visiting services have been provided by various agencies over decades, the potential of this approach has been largely overlooked. There is much still to be learned about the impact of home visiting. Questions of interest include the similarities and differences between paid and volunteer home visitors, and the role of the visitor's local networks as a resource for families. Another issue is the need to go beyond home visiting so families engage in activities of mutual support once trust has been established.

Encouraging the development of partnerships between families and schools has been another approach of agencies with a concern for community building and enhancing the safety and wellbeing of children. Particularly in areas of socioeconomic disadvantage, there may be a tradition of parents feeling rejected and intimidated by schools. There are many benefits for children when families are able to develop open and trusting relationships with school staff. Parents and teachers are better able to discuss concerns and develop a consistent approach. Children feel more positive about learning if they see their parents are comfortable about their school. Schools benefit from the time and skills parents bring. Strategies for promoting closer ties between home and school include organising social functions for families and staff, using the school as a base for community activities and groups, and schools actively identifying and using the skills and resources of parents.

There are financial costs in community-building strategies. These include the cost of physical infrastructure and of human resources, particularly in areas where stocks of social capital are low. The belief is, however, that a financial investment in strengthening communities now will ultimately reduce the costs of social dislocation and child abuse in the longer term.

COMMUNITY BUILDING AND DOMESTIC VIOLENCE

Although little has been written explicitly about the relationship between community building and domestic violence, several key strategies in addressing domestic violence can also be seen as having an impact on the generation of social capital.

The process of identifying domestic violence has involved the creation and promotion of new norms around violence in relationships.

In the past a range of beliefs helped to legitimise or hide violence in families. These included beliefs about the roles and rights of men, beliefs about acceptable ways of expressing anger and stereotypes about women. These beliefs were reinforced by powerful institutions in the community, such as the police and the courts of law.

Although evidence of these beliefs can still be seen, new norms about relationships are being promoted across communities. Community education campaigns promote such ideas as 'real men don't bash women' and 'violence is a crime' with posters, pamphlets and television advertisements. Within the legal system strategies have been developed to assist family members who want to take steps against violence occurring in the home. Resources, such as accommodation, have been organised to assist women leaving violent situations and support services for women taking court action have been established. These strategies are evidence of changing norms and also a means by which new norms are strengthened. In spite of the ongoing challenge of promoting safety within families, the changes which have occurred in only two decades are immense.

It is worth reflecting on the strategies by which norms about domestic violence have been challenged, and considering the work still to be done. The earliest responses to domestic violence, such as the first women's refuges, were outside formal social structures, since these structures tended to support the old norms that excused violence in families. The police often discounted violence in the home as 'just a domestic' and the legal system had different rules for violence within a marriage and violence elsewhere. The 'discovery' of domestic violence came not primarily as part of an organised social inquiry but as a consequence of a wider questioning of the role of women. Early actions, such as setting up refuges for women escaping violence, were created from partnerships between women who had a personal experience of violence and those who had a political commitment to creating alternatives. The processes that led to the provision of government funding for a range of services and the development of legal options to promote safety came much later, in response to the emergence of new norms. These new possibilities resulted from pressure applied by groups on the outside of goverment and influence exerted by people within government and government departments.

Within the community there is still a range of views about domestic violence. It is evident that isolation helps maintain old norms that influence people who act violently and those who are affected by violence. If people are isolated from the opportunity to discuss their ideas and reactions to such issues, the impact of media campaigns will be reduced.

Providing services where families are affected by violence does not automatically lead to a change in the attitudes that support violent behaviour. As workers in the field are painfully aware, perpetrators may cease the behaviour that is subject to legal sanctions, such as physical assault, while remaining violent in other ways that are beyond the influence of the law, such as total control over household finances and restricting contact with family and friends. A continuing challenge is to consolidate new norms in relation to family violence through the development of a broad community consensus. Addressing such issues from a community-building approach raises broader questions, such as whether it is more effective to focus solely on the negative behaviour that needs to stop, or whether the process of changing norms would be enhanced by consideration of the preferred behaviour.

COMMUNITY BUILDING AND POVERTY

A range of commentators have suggested that stocks of social capital are a necessary precursor for the development of economic capital. At the most basic level, some degree of trust is necessary to enable people to develop a system of money and to be able to lend and borrow. But the implications of social capital for the wealth of a community may go much further than that. Social interactions that contribute to the development of networks embedded in the community also act as conduits for economic activity. For example, if someone has something to sell, the more people they know, the more potential buyers they can contact. Similarly, people with an extensive social network will be able to use their contacts as an asset if they are looking for a job for themselves or a member of their family. Groups of families can band together to increase their purchasing power. For example, organising a fruit and vegetable cooperative that can buy in bulk from the wholesale markets can enable a group of families to obtain nutritious food more cheaply than they could as individuals. Because of the suggested links with financial capital, even organisations such as the World Bank are keenly interested in the study of social capital.

While it has been suggested that social capital may be needed to develop a financial infrastructure, in communities that are significantly disadvantaged, external financial resources may be needed to initiate the kinds of activities that generate social capital. This could mean the provision of a safe place for families to meet or workers whose role is to act in collaboration with local people not to direct families into the kinds of activities outsiders believe will be of benefit to them. For some families, the effects of financial disadvantage may be so acute that without some targeted assistance, such as accessible transport or subsidies so that their children can participate in activities with their peers, the barriers to wider participation in neighbourhood activities will remain in place.

Even when resources such as community centres are built, the providers are not necessarily concerned about how they will be used to bring people together, but who will manage them. There is sometimes an assumption that the opportunity for community-based management in itself will be a transforming experience. Recognising the impact of low social capital helps to explain why community development can get stuck at this point. If people living in the neighbourhood do not know each other, if they are not sure what to expect from others and if they find it hard to trust each other, the whole notion of collaborating around management is likely to be irrelevant.

CHALLENGES FOR WORKERS USING THE COMMUNITY-BUILDING APPROACH

Taking time to think about the big picture

An awareness of social capital encourages family workers to think about the wider context of their work and in particular the ongoing development of their community. For workers who are constantly confronted with families in crisis, it may seem difficult or even impossible to take time away from immediate concerns, such as children at risk of abuse, to give priority to activities that are directed at community building. These immediate concerns may also be of little interest to funding bodies.

However, if no consideration is given to community-building activities, families are less likely to have access to the resources that can contribute to their effective functioning. This is especially true for communities where there is significant socioeconomic disadvantage. It is difficult for volunteer groups to mobilise support and identify the capacities of residents feeling stigmatised by the reputation of their community without at least an initial injection of external resources and skills.

As this chapter has identified, awareness of the potential for developing social capital can prompt family workers to adapt at least some existing activities to incorporate greater opportunities for social interaction. Family workers should also consider the need to communicate the rationale for such activities to management and other agencies.

Stretching resources

Activities that generate social capital will require time and effort to plan, implement and review. As initiatives gain momentum there are likely to be expanded opportunities for local residents to play an active role. While this should be an affirming and energising experience, if participants are over-burdened they may end up feeling drained, exploited and disillusioned. Paid staff might experience difficulties balancing an awareness of the need to support unpaid workers who are involved in their community with those activities for which the organisation receives funding, such as providing counselling and running groups. A further complication might occur if an unpaid worker is experiencing challenges within their family while they are being relied upon as a resource for the community.

An additional dilemma for smaller services can involve their limited capacity to engage with more than a few people in their locality. This may restrict their ability to find people who can contribute strengths to community-building activities and may raise concerns about the impact of very small-scale activities.

Clearly cooperation between formal and informal groups with a family focus offers the possibility to increase the impact of community-building efforts. At the same time, bringing together organisations with different ways of working can be time consuming. Without clear purpose, sometimes bringing a group together becomes an end in itself, without contributing to a greater sense of trust and proactivity between participants.

Realistic expectations

Social capital has existed for as long as people have done things co-operatively. An awareness of social capital may assist us to understand better where community work gets stuck and may provide alternative approaches to working with communities with limited resources. Effective tools to measure and compare social capital will be immensely valuable.

At the same time, social capital is not a magic wand for community building. While social capital enhances cooperative endeavours, issues of inequity and competing interests remain an integral part of community life. It can be predicted that there will be less conflict where stores of social capital are increased, but there are no guarantees that conflict will not arise.

Increased recognition of the value of community building should not be taken to undermine the validity of community development strategies that emphasise the provision of infrastructure or taking direct action. An awareness of social capital can be especially useful when workers experience difficulty generating an interest in other community development strategies. Its value is diminished where it is invested with mystical or unrealistic properties.

GETTING INVOLVED: KELLY'S STORY

Kelly's story is about her involvement in Shared Action, a community development project in her local neighbourhood.

Kelly's story shows:

- the importance of building trust and self-esteem
- an engagement in activities based on reciprocity and mutuality
- the encouragement of diversity.

> I first heard about Shared Action when I was at playgroup one day. The playgroup was at the community house just across the road from my house. Linda (the Shared Action worker) asked me if I would like to become involved as a volunteer. The people seemed nice so I went to a couple of meetings. You could either get to the meetings yourself or people drove you. I didn't know what they might want me to do, but one of the first things they were doing was looking at the history of our area. I've lived here all my life and my parents and relatives have always lived around here. I know lots of people so I thought I might be able to be part of the history group. I can't read or write but that didn't matter. I didn't usually join things like this because I wouldn't be sure that I would be welcome. I used to go to some things at the community house because my parents who were living next

door to me had done a lot of things to get it going a long time ago.

Shared Action had a community barbecue in the park. I asked my dad to do the cooking. The park is very close to my place, so I could go home and get anything that was needed. At Shared Action we had volunteer name tags. You didn't have to do everything with Shared Action, just the bits that you were interested in and available for. The name tags made you feel more confident.

Another thing Shared Action was doing was visiting the schools to talk to the teachers about the project and to get them involved. My first daughter had started school, so Linda asked me if I would like to be in the group to visit her school. We talked about some Shared Action ideas. I would never have done this except for Shared Action because I didn't like schools. I went to a special school and one of my teachers there said one day that any children I might have would also go to a special school. I didn't like that. I decided they wouldn't.

I was happy my daughter was at a normal school and I wanted to do everything I could to help her stay there. Then one day she came home and begged me to volunteer to work in the school canteen. At first I didn't want to. I was scared they might not want me because I can't read and write. But I didn't want to let her down. So I plucked up all my courage and went to the school. I thought they would laugh but the lady in the office knew me through Shared Action by now and said it didn't matter if I couldn't read, they would help if I needed it. I like it in the canteen. I can do the work and have to work with lots of different parents. I got to know all the teachers, and most of the kids know whose mother I am. I have got two going to school there now and they are proud of me.

I used to work there often but now I can only do it once a month because I go to my own school. Last year Shared Action started a group where parents, teachers and children came together after school once a week to practise ideas about helping children with school work. Me and my kids went. One day there a lady was talking about adult literacy. I thought about the idea of going back to school but usually people laugh at you if you can't read. But I wanted to be able to help my girls do well at school so I plucked up all my courage again and went and had a look. I was amazed to see the people there—older people and all sorts of people. I decided to start the course. It is good fun and everybody helps each other. I go there three days a week. I'm surprised I like it so much and I am very surprised that I feel okay about going to the girls' school. I feel pretty comfortable with the teachers and I feel part of the place. I know I am helpful at the school. I hated school when I was a kid.

I think reading and writing will help me in lots of ways, but particularly to help my children enjoy school and do well. My youngest girl starts kindergarten next year.

It is not as hard to be involved in things when you feel more confident and that you can be accepted. I feel braver to say what I think, and people reckon I am a good mother. I like living here and working to help with things like the building of the park.

FINDING OUT MORE

Community building is a broad term to describe recent attempts to strengthen community support networks and develop community capacities. The emerging community-building literature is often concerned more with strategies than theoretical issues, although ideas about social capital have provided some theoretical base. These ideas are complemented by literature applying a strengths-based perspective to community development and research linking the social supports available in neighbourhoods to the capacity of families to care for their children.

Bullen, Paul, with Onyx, Jenny (1999) *Social Capital: Family Support Services and Neighbourhood and Community Centres in NSW*, Management Alternatives, Sydney. A comparison of social capital stocks across a range of populations, this study highlights implications for organisations seeking to build social capital while providing services.

Cox, Eva (1995) *A Truly Civil Society*, ABC Books, Sydney. Cox argues that informal networks should be recognised alongside formal associations in the creation of social capital.

Garbarino, James, and Kostelny, Kathleen (1994) 'Family Support and Community Development' in Kagan, Sharon, and Weissbourd, Bernice (eds) *Putting Families First: America's Family Support Movement and the Challenge of Change*, Jossey-Bass, San Francisco. The significance of social support for children and families is outlined by Garbarino and Kostelny, with particular attention on the significance of trust and norms in neighbourhoods and communities.

Kretzman, John, and McKnight, John (1993) *Building Communities from the Inside Out*, ACTA Publications, Chicago. This book provides a wealth of ways in which the assets of communities, including formal and informal networks, can be mobilised.

Putnam, Robert (1993) 'The Prosperous Community: Social Capital and Public Life', *American Prospect*, 13: 35–42. Putnam was one of the first people to describe the elements of social capital and link it to the concept of the civil society.

seven

Working within
one approach

When I started working at this agency, we were overwhelmed with people's problems. We reported on problems, we talked about problems, we were there to advocate for problems. There were all these families where there was no expectation of change in their situation. Then we made a deliberate decision to change the way we worked. Now we have something to do when people are ready to move on from telling their story. We're not just there to see how people are going. We're celebrating their achievements. (Robyn, service coordinator)

Workers like Robyn see an optimistic approach as more than just another resource in their tool kit. They have decided to give one approach a particular priority in their work. They may describe this by saying that their work is 'informed' by a particular approach or that they 'work within' a particular approach. This may be a personal choice made by an individual worker or one made by a team. Working within a specific approach does not mean that workers are cut off from all other ideas in their work. It does mean that when workers ask themselves the question 'What do I do next?', they draw on their core approach to think about the process of change.

This chapter focuses on what happens when workers or organisations decide to focus on a particular approach in family work.

These ideas can apply to approaches other than the four detailed in this book. They apply to all approaches that are relevant to family work. These ideas are informed by an optimistic stance that change can happen and it can only come where families' capacities are mobilised.

IMPROVING PRACTICE BY WORKING WITHIN A SPECIFIC APPROACH

Families can make change happen regardless of, or even in spite of, the beliefs and practices of workers. However, working consistently within a specific approach can assist workers to identify and avoid practices that get in the way of change, and to be more alert to possibilities for change.

Working with individual families

Working within one particular optimistic approach can assist workers to address some significant challenges in work with individual families. Because family workers are generally skilled non-judgemental listeners, families may be able to tell their story and feel heard in a way they have not experienced before. For some families, this in itself may open up new possibilities. But for other families the warmth and acceptance they experience with the worker leads to the expectation that the family worker will be there as their friend or even as a parent figure. Once this expectation is established it is difficult for the worker to move outside this role without seeming to reject the family. Workers find themselves feeling anxious as they see evidence that the family is becoming dependent on them, and that family members have expectations that they will be unable to meet.

While listening to the family's story is always important, using an optimistic approach as a reference point encourages workers not to rely just on the quality of their relationship with the family as the vehicle of change. A worker employing an optimistic approach looks from the beginning for strategic opportunities to explore possibilities for the future. Such an approach also assists workers to avoid creating dependence by placing their actions in a context that emphasises the family's role, rather than their own.

Sometimes family workers feel like nothing is working. They may become locked into unhelpful patterns of interaction, such as blaming the family or seeking to rescue them. Working within an optimistic approach does not guarantee that workers will avoid such difficulties, but it can help workers to maintain a respectful stance towards the family and to review their work in a way that may open up a different way to proceed.

> We got to the stage where tea and empathy were not enough. We recognised that we wanted to be involved in change. (Catherine, service coordinator)

> I find now I'm better able to identify priorities. If something's getting in the way, like a family always finding excuses for why things won't work, I can find ways to respond. (Vinnie, family worker)

> If you don't know where you're going, you can end up meeting the expectation that you are just like a friend. Having a clear approach gives you a bigger or clearer picture about how change can happen. It's liberating to feel that you don't have to have all the answers. (Eva, family worker)

Working as a team

Sometimes team members make a deliberate decision to adopt a particular approach or over time the majority of workers develop a shared interest in a common approach. Members of such teams report that having a shared understanding of how their work fosters change can enable them to support and challenge each other more effectively. By making their ideas about change explicit, they are better able to identify where colleagues may have become stuck, and to critique each other's work, reducing defensiveness about or fear of admitting mistakes.

Sharing an approach also provides a common language for team members to discuss any difficulties they may have working together. Using the same approach to change for themselves as they do for families can help staff consolidate their skills in family work. It ensures that their attempts to maximise possibilities for change with families are not undermined by ways of working within the team that contradict the processes on which their work with families is based.

> Just as in our work with families we listen for stories, in team meetings we've identified stories of criticism and looked for alternative stories. (Family Support Service, Newcastle)

In staff meetings we look at giving feedback to each other focusing on our strengths. If there is an issue, like self-care for members of the team, we set up ways that people on the team can contribute. We also use the same goal-setting approach to staff appraisals that we would use with families. (Family Support Service, Deniliquin)

Using a common approach also encourages workers to evaluate all their work practices in the light of their shared beliefs about fostering change. When ideas about the process of change are made explicit, workers sometimes find that practices they had taken for granted do not fit well with those beliefs. This challenges workers to ensure that not only their individual work but their whole service reflects their beliefs about working with families. While this kind of self–assessment is not unique to teams with a shared framework, team members report that the shared framework increases their awareness of contradictions in what they are doing and gives them more confidence in developing new practices.

We got rid of our parenting skills group, because we started to question the idea that what made a difference to parenting was just skills. We now call the group 'Living with Children' and our focus is sharing the struggle. We've become more open to the knowledge people already have. (Susanna, family worker at a child protection service)

We've developed different practices for record keeping, to reflect our overall approach. Families have a folder in their home where notes from sessions are kept. These focus on the family's goals, strengths and the strategies that have been identified during the session. The folder also includes a statement about confidentiality and a sheet the family can use to give us feedback at any time. We use letters to the family when we want a record to be held by us and the family. The fact that the family holds the folder emphasises that the process is about addressing the family's needs, not fitting the family into the service. (Robyn, service coordinator)

I'm not necessarily doing things differently. But I am doing them with more confidence. I'm more assertive and I speak up faster than I did in the past. (Tirrania, service coordinator)

Some services also report that working within a shared approach can change the way that their work is viewed by other services. While this was not their motivation for moving towards a shared approach, they found people took their work more seriously, and were more ready to recognise their competence because it was perceived that they had an underlying rationale for working in the way they did. This change was particularly noticeable because some family workers had previously felt that other services were only prepared to acknowledge the concrete assistance and emotional support they gave families, but did not recognise family work, especially in the family's home, as having the potential to focus on change. Once this aspect of their work was better recognised they felt their picture of the family was also given more credence. While this set up the risk that recognition of workers' expertise might be at the expense of an acknowledgement of the family's understanding of their situation, workers appreciated being taken seriously by colleagues.

> Having expertise in this approach gave us a credibility we hadn't had before. (Theresa, agency manager)

> Often in the community sector you feel that you're in a victim position. You're always one down. It can really affect you personally. Now I find I can work as an equal with people I use to be in awe of. (Tirrania, service coordinator)

Choosing an approach to work within

Many workers who have chosen to specialise in one approach suggest that they feel a particular affinity with the approach they have chosen. There is a sense in which the approach touches a chord with them and enables them to put their values into practice more completely. They may also see a particular fit between the approach and their role in family work.

> I find cognitive work fits well into work in the family's home. Families can identify readily with the idea of self-talk. Because you're not going into the past, you don't run the risk of raising emotions which could be hard for a parent to deal with in a situation where after the session they are at home with the children on their own. (Catherine, service coordinator)

> I was attracted to the sense of discovery with narrative, the sense of not being the expert. I liked the fact that narrative didn't push people into what they weren't ready for, and the ways questions opened out people's views rather than closing things off. (Margaret, adolescent and family worker)

> I went to a conference on the solution-focused approach and it made sense. I thought there and then, 'I'm going back to work to start putting things back to the family'. (Robyn, service coordinator)

Other factors in deciding to work within one approach are access to training and ongoing support from others working within the same approach. These are particularly important for approaches that emphasise ideas about direct work with families, as is the case with cognitive, narrative and solution-focused work. While reading a book or attending a one-day workshop can be a beginning, they probably will not be enough to consolidate learning. Agencies are likely to find that they need to direct their available staff development resources toward workers developing their competence in the specific approach, rather than spreading resources across a range of topics. As staff develop more competence they may be able to address the training needs of new staff more effectively within the team's resources.

Where a team decides to adopt a shared approach, it is preferable for all members of the team to have training. If a small group of staff receive training and are eager to convert others, staff who have not had the opportunity may understandably feel resentful, particularly if they have difficulty understanding what the excitement is all about.

Offering training to staff in specialist roles can heighten the sense that some positions are seen as more valuable to the agency than others. If workers feel that new ideas are being imposed from above and that their expertise is being devalued, positive change is less likely.

Training should present the approach in a way that applies to the settings in which family work is undertaken. Family workers are often in contact with families in their home or a mix of settings. They may be working with families who have been directed to attend the service by a court or statutory body. Workers will find it easier to see how new ideas make a difference if their work setting is taken into account, rather than if they are expected to adapt ideas and examples from a very different context.

Since family workers often work in community-based services with limited access to resources for training, they may need to think laterally about how to gain access to training and support. This is a special challenge for services in rural areas where travel is a significant component of costs. Strategies to address these difficulties include:

• encouraging other agencies in one town to share the costs of bringing in an outside presenter to provide training

- cooperative arrangements with staff from different agencies attending a course together
- looking for larger agencies that might be willing to provide staff to provide supervision or train local staff.

The learning process

Learning anything new takes time and learning a new approach to family work is no exception. In the early stages workers may find they feel awkward or artificial, and it can be difficult working out whether this is because the ideas do not fit or because they are unfamiliar. It can be helpful to know that this is a common experience, and that it is not unusual for people to go through a stage of feeling less competent than they felt before they started using the new approach.

> When I first started using the new approach I felt like I was being deskilled. It was very hard to move from saying 'What is the problem here?' At the moment I think consciously about what I will do next, but I am hoping it will feel more natural over time. (Eva, family worker)

> I found it hard at first to cope with the vocabulary. Other people's questions wouldn't fit with me. (Linda, adolescent counsellor)

Learning a new approach will not necessarily be simple or a matter of comfortably adding new skills to old ones. Workers build up habitual patterns which sometimes they must give up as they become more familiar with optimistic approaches to working with families.

> I had to stop giving advice and trying to explain everything. In the beginning I was fearful of missing something, which I guess was that feeling that I still had to be the expert. (Kerry, adolescent counsellor)

> You have to put aside comfortableness and cosiness, and take on a willingness to be examined. (Annette, service coordinator)

A significant moment comes when workers find work with a family particularly challenging. At this point they can expect to feel the temptation to return to more familiar ways of working. An indication that they have developed a preferred approach is the willingness to persist with the approach when they feel stuck, as well as at times when its application is easier.

As time goes on workers can expect to feel more natural about their use of the approach. At this point they tend to describe their approach more in terms of a way of being or of viewing situations, rather than as a set of techniques. What also becomes evident is a readiness to apply the ideas used with families to a wider sphere, including to situations affecting the worker personally, without feeling self-conscious.

> It's taken about twelve months for me to be able to do it naturally. The hardest thing was letting families direct things differently from the way I felt I would. (Tina, family worker)

> I'll never have it exactly the same way as in the books. But I know now that even though you fumble, if you've got the way of thinking, there will be an outcome. (Sue, group worker)

The implications of developing a new approach might not be felt just by workers. If families have experienced workers taking control of their lives in the past, they may be taken aback when they find workers are no longer assuming the role of the expert.

> Sometimes families would say, 'This doesn't feel like therapy. Are you sure it will work? When am I going to get the list of what I have to do?' (Raylene, family worker)

> We had a powerful role in people's lives and they formed very dependent relationships. We were always doing things for people, and even when we tried to give responsibility back to people, they would still ask us why we hadn't rung. It took time to stop giving people solutions. (Robyn, service coordinator)

CHALLENGES OF WORKING WITHIN ONE APPROACH

Remembering the basics about what helps families

It is vital that workers do not lose track of the fundamental assumptions about working with families, outlined in chapter 1. These are at the heart of all family work, regardless of the specific approach taken. The building blocks on which all family work is based include:

- starting where the family is
- building respectful relationships

- setting goals or outcomes
- helping in practical ways when needed
- building networks
- building on strengths.

Nothing can justify disrespect, taking control of the lives of families or being dismissive of families or colleagues.

Not allowing the approach to have a limiting effect

Working within a specific approach should not feel like a straight-jacket. While it is usual for workers to feel some anxiety as they are becoming familiar with a new approach, the pressure to 'do it right' can get in the way of developing competence. This is especially true if workers feel they have to duplicate the style of work of others, regardless of the fit with the family or themselves.

Workers may also react to this kind of pressure by cutting them-selves off from anything that does not wear the brand name of their preferred approach. As a result, workers run the risk of missing out on relevant ideas that share common ground with their preferred approach, even if they do not wear the label. Withdrawing from the kinds of discussions that take place in training sessions and confer-ences among family workers in general also means workers miss out on the opportunity to critique new ideas from their particular per-spective. If they do not participate in broad discussion, they will not be in a position to develop an understanding of the ideas influencing the practice of other workers in the community.

Focusing on the strengths of the family, not the strengths of the approach

It is possible for workers to become caught up in the strategies and techniques of their preferred approach. This can lead them, some-times quite unconsciously, to attribute responsibility for change to the approach rather than to the family. Workers may then discount change the family has achieved if it took place outside the influence of their preferred approach, failing to pay attention to changes the family has made on their own. Such attitudes might lead workers to put down work done with another worker, even where the family perceives aspects of that work to have been useful.

It is interesting to note that the families' stories that conclude chapters 3–6 share common themes. Each highlights the family member's emerging sense of self-worth, and the growth of mastery and confidence in their situation. The processes of change may vary, but in the final analysis, change that persists is change, regardless of the approach used by the worker. The role of workers is to honour change in the life of families, rather than to seek to promote their own contribution to the process of change at the expense of others.

To date, research comparing different approaches to family work has been limited. Studies from formal therapeutic settings have been inconclusive, although it has been argued that the factors most strongly associated with change are shared by a number of approaches, rather than monopolised by one. These factors include establishing a trusting collaboration between worker and family, building on strengths rather than focusing on deficits and nurturing a sense of optimism (Snyder et al. 1999; Bachelor and Horvath 1999).

If this is so, it suggests that the value of an optimistic approach may be in keeping workers focused on the family's view of their needs and experiences, and assisting workers to avoid fitting the family's situation into their own ideas about family difficulties or needs. An optimistic approach makes workers alert to the family's contribution to the process of change and helps them to avoid blaming, defeatist practices that are discouraging to both families and workers alike.

Keeping the big picture in view

Family workers and agencies that are influenced by a specific approach are usually attracted to that approach because they can see how it will improve their practice with families. They are more likely to be attracted to approaches that obviously relate to individuals and families, such as the solution-focused, narrative and cognitive approaches.

The particular challenge to workers and organisations using one of these approaches is to incorporate ideas developed in a community context, such as the community-building approach. When thinking about change workers need to consider the community resources on which a family can draw. It can be argued that the community-building approach is a vital component of any effective family work initiatives.

ONCE A FAMILY HAS MADE ONE CHANGE . . .

Jan is a family worker with a Family Support Service. Her story highlights:

*   the challenges of working within a new approach
*   the awareness of leaving some practices behind
*   the way in which her attention is focused on change.

I've been working as a family worker for eleven years. Before the team started finding out about this approach, we were bogged down. We stayed with families a long time. In fact, now I would say we were nurturing their problems. It was hard in the beginning because we were trying to learn from other people in the service who'd been to workshops. We had to develop our own technique and after a while the ideas just came, even when I wouldn't have dreamed before of using them.

In a crisis I'm not conscious of the approach. I need to do the practical stuff first. That might mean working with the family to find housing, or to deal with debts because the sheriff is at the door. As you're doing that there's space for the family's story to emerge.

I found I had to stop continually going over old stuff with people. I've learned how to move on without cutting people off. I've learned that change is a process and it won't happen all at once. But once a family has made one change, more change is likely to come.

eight

Beyond technique: optimism in practice

Ahmed reaches for the phone with one hand and flicks through a pile of papers with the other. One month into his job as a child protection officer, he is at a loss to know what to do about Jenny, aged four, and Vince, aged two. A neighbour called the child protection department when Vince was found wandering along the road after dark.

Vanessa Nguyen, Vince's mother, says she is trying to manage. But since her boyfriend ripped her off and left her to cope with his debts, some days she feels so down she just stays in bed. She cannot face the supermarket, so most of the time the family eat baked beans from the corner shop. The children spend most of the day sitting in front of the television. Ahmed has spent time talking to Vanessa and he has made some suggestions about things she could do. At the time she agrees, but when he goes back to the house nothing has happened. She came to the country in her early teens as a refugee and she has no family to call on. Yesterday she said she felt like she was at a deadend with nowhere to go. Ahmed's manager has suggested he refer Vanessa to the family centre. Ahmed wonders what a family worker could do to help this family. Is there any hope that things can change?

Ahmed has asked a good question. How can family work contribute to change? Why do family workers do what they do?

There are some immediate steps that all competent family workers are likely to take when meeting Vanessa, regardless of their particular ideas about change. These would include establishing a rapport with family members, looking for indications of significant safety concerns relating to Vanessa or the children and searching for immediate ways to take pressure off the family. Depending on Vanessa's situation, the worker might negotiate to follow-up some of these steps to help get things started for Vanessa. But beyond this, how do workers foster the process of change?

WORKING WITHIN A SPECIFIC APPROACH

As chapter 7 outlined, some family workers would draw on one particular approach as a starting point in answering Ahmed's question.

Brenda, who works from a narrative approach, might say:

> Listening to the description of Vanessa's story it sounds like there are lots of ways in which she's been pushed around and ripped off. Focusing on that story it's not surprising that things seem as if they are stuck at a deadend. What I would be interested in are the other stories that have been lost because the story about Vanessa being a dead loss has been getting so much airplay. Like the story of a child who landed in a new country as a refugee and has had to do it on her own. And the story of someone who has been ripped off but hasn't gone under. I'd be encouraging some more of those stories to emerge, and finding out what they say about Vanessa and the things about herself that the deadend story has blotted out.

Brenda is focusing on the emergence of alternative stories in the expectation that as those stories emerge Vanessa's view of herself will change. As she starts to see herself as 'writing a new story', new possibilities can become available for her and her children.

Ray, who uses a solution-focused approach, might say:

> Rather than giving Vanessa more suggestions of things she could do, I'd like to spend some time finding out about any times when things haven't been so bad. That might mean finding out if some days are better than others or finding out what things were like before the difficulties she's facing at the moment took hold. We'd start looking at what Vanessa might be doing at these times, when

the problems weren't so evident. We'd be looking for a small goal to start with and some solutions that come from Vanessa's ideas and experience. Say if Vanessa remembered that one morning last week she did get out of bed first thing, we'd find out what she did to achieve that and how she could do it again. We'd also explore what strengths Vanessa has drawn on in her life and we'd look at how she might be able to mobilise these more now. We'd be starting small, but that's okay because once people achieve some small changes they find that bigger changes can come more easily.

The solution-focused approach to change emphasises exceptions to the problem, rather than encouraging exploration of the problem.

Ann, who uses a cognitive approach, might say:

As I talked to Vanessa I'd be listening out for the kinds of thoughts that contribute to her feeling more stuck or don't fit with the facts. We'd spend some time examining one of those thoughts and looking at what Vanessa is saying to herself when those thoughts take hold. We'd focus on thoughts that could be helpful as a way of countering thoughts that don't help. This is a strategy that Vanessa can learn to do for herself. We might also identify the kinds of beliefs that fuel those thoughts and applying the same strategies that work for countering those thoughts to countering those beliefs. Once Vanessa can challenge unhelpful beliefs and thoughts for herself, she may find she is better able to use strategies for tackling problems that have worked for her in the past. We can explore those strategies and, if she finds there are gaps, we can work on developing skills to address those areas.

Ann's focus in fostering change is on Vanessa's 'self-talk' and the development of responses that challenge messages that are not accurate or are not working for her.

Brenda, Ray and Ann all see finding opportunities for developing social capital as underlying all the work that they do. They would be looking for opportunities for Vanessa, Jenny and Vince to develop links with people and services in their local community. They would also expect that the more Vanessa sees herself as a worthwhile person, the more experience she has of trusting relationships—both with paid staff and other families she meets at the family centre—and the more life skills she develops, the stronger those links will be.

Li sees her service primarily as working with families through community building, rather than individual work. She sees developing social capital as an essential base for community change. She comments:

> Although we are primarily a community development program, we are often the first place people come to when they feel stuck, because we are easy to find and our centre is family-friendly. We might see someone like Vanessa at crisis point, but we have good contacts with a range of agencies that would be able to work with the family on an individual basis if that seems to be appropriate in the longer term.
>
> We recognise how hard it is for families to feel comfortable with new services, and we'd try to accompany them to the early appointments until they feel safe. We can also offer Vanessa and her children opportunities to develop links with other families. Often this works best early on if it's through a structured group, where the group leader can facilitate the development of trust and assist members to practise new skills. By attending child care while Vanessa attends a group, Jenny and Vince can also have new experiences and make friends with the child carers and other children. Later on Vanessa might become involved in an ongoing group, such as a playgroup, where she can both develop friendships that extend beyond the group and contribute to the life of her community.

ADDING ON TO A CORE APPROACH

Some workers have a core approach, but they also draw on other approaches to change when such approaches seem to offer something that complements their usual approach or something that fits with a particular situation.

> Rita's team have a strong commitment to working within a narrative approach, but members of the team have also had some training in solution-focused work. Rita comments, 'Because Vanessa is feeling very stuck, sometimes we would start off using a solution-focused approach, because in our experience this can help families experience small changes quite quickly. Once Vanessa has put some solutions in place to address the family's most urgent goals, there's some space for alternative stories to emerge.' Rita adds, 'New staff sometimes find solution-focused ideas easier to grasp in the beginning and as they become more experienced they are

able to use narrative ideas more. As a team, narrative is the approach we would use when we think about the bigger picture for families or for ourselves.'

Brian has a background in cognitive work, but more recently he has been using solution-focused ideas. Brian feels it is important to be aware of the assumptions underlying whatever approach the worker is using and he is wary of using bits and pieces: 'I keep asking myself, "Where did this idea come from?" . . . I like the respectful way solution-focused ideas help to establish a collaborative relationship. I would be very aware of that with Vanessa, because while it's easy to offer advice when someone is feeling overwhelmed, I know that what will really make a difference are solutions which she has identified. I sometimes use some cognitive strategies once the family has identified goals to work on. For example, if Vanessa decided she wanted to spend less time staying in bed, we might use charting thought responses or activities in the course of working towards this goal.'

DRAWING ON A NUMBER OF APPROACHES

Some workers say they prefer not to be limited to one approach to change. They prefer to be exposed to a range of ideas and then to choose what seems appropriate for a particular family.

Susi describes herself as pluralist. She says her core values are humanistic, focusing on the value of the individual, and beyond that she concentrates on understanding the family's story and starting where the family is right now. 'I would start by developing a relationship with Vanessa, and finding out what was the most important thing for her. I would spend time looking at things she might want to change in her life, and we would look at breaking those goals down into achievable steps. I'd be looking at the messages Vanessa's got about herself over the years, and we'd also look at ways of raising her self-esteem. I couldn't tell you exactly where the ideas I use come from, but however you use them the family have to be at the centre. I also think once people make some small changes you get a ripple effect into other areas of their life.'

Nada sees herself as having an ecological approach: 'I'd be interested in the influences on the family, so that I can understand their particular context. I'm strongly influenced by feminist ideas, so I'd be looking at Vanessa's experiences and ways in which her status as a woman have shaped her experiences and her view of herself. I'd be looking at ways in which an awareness of this could change her view of herself and her options. We'd talk about her strategies for managing the children and how her own parenting experiences have shaped these. That can open up discussion of what she wants for her kids. When she's feeling more confident I'd encourage her to get involved in one of the groups our centre runs. I'd expect that meeting other women in similar situations would help her to value herself more and give her a new perspective on her role as a parent.'

Arguments about the validity of drawing from a range of approaches can raise strong feelings among workers who have different viewpoints.

Toni, who works within one specific approach, expresses it this way: 'I feel very concerned about workers just focusing on techniques, taking a bit from here and a bit from there. You can end up not really understanding the underlying assumptions and process. It's also really confusing for families if workers are slipping between different metaphors all the time.'

Gemma, who sees herself as drawing on lots of approaches, says: 'I don't want to be limited to one approach in fostering change. In fact I feel that someone else telling me what I should do undermines some of the assumptions on which these approaches are based. They wouldn't prescribe to a family what they can and can't do, and so it doesn't seem consistent to tell me what I can and can't do either. At the end of the day it's up to the family to decide whether the worker's approach is helpful.'

Such debates rarely result in converts. One result of such disagreements can be for people to become even more entrenched in their positions. At worst, such strong feelings are raised that respect and openness can go out the window, making it impossible for dialogue to continue. This is unfortunate, because the value of optimistic approaches such as those outlined in this book is not that they contain some special kind of magic. None of these approaches offers a formula that can be applied to families to promote change regardless of the family's participation. Nor will the techniques that are informed by these approaches make a difference if workers using them are preoccupied with their view of what the family needs, or if they believe that the family cannot change and that others must do the work for them.

This book suggests that the value of optimistic approaches is that they encourage workers to look beyond their beliefs about what the family needs and focus on the world from the family's point of view. They also highlight what family members experience as helpful, without necessitating an exhaustive review of what has gone wrong in the family's life. This keeps the worker and the family oriented to possibilities for change, rather than focusing on where the family has fallen short of their own or others' expectations.

DEVELOPING OPTIMISTIC PRACTICE

By focusing on characteristics of optimistic practice it is possible for workers to assess their own work, regardless of whether they use one approach or a combination. The following questions reflect the assumption that for workers to be optimistic in their work with families they need not only to believe that change is possible, and that it is based on the capacities of families not workers, they also need to be able to put these beliefs into practice in their work.

There are often many valid reasons for family workers to have negative feelings about what family members have done or said. Family workers may themselves be subject to abuse or harassment. They might witness family members behaving in an abusive way to others. They may see the impact of adults' behaviour on children while others minimise or excuse actions the worker believes are harmful. It is not helpful for family workers to believe they must pretend to feel positive when they do not, or to feel that they will be criticised if they verbalise their frustration or anger about family members' actions.

Differing individuals and teams will develop varying strategies for addressing these kinds of situations. The impact of an optimistic stance is not that family workers never feel negative, but that they don't only feel negative. The following questions have been developed as a resource for workers in practising optimism.

Are you working as if change is possible for this family?

I believe in people before they believe in themselves. (Gaye, family worker)

The belief that change cannot happen fundamentally affects workers' effectiveness with the family and with communities. There may be aspects of a family's life that will not change, such as a family member with a disability or a chronic illness. There may be well-established patterns of behaviour that family members may find very hard to change. Structural factors have a significant impact on communities. But if family workers believe that nothing can change, they will not be looking for small changes that could have a bigger significance. Their pessimism can end up helping to confirm the sense of hopelessness that is already felt in the family or in the community.

It is not enough for workers to believe in a theoretical way that change is possible. The way they work with families communicates more powerfully than words whether workers are anticipating change. The more workers find themselves doing things for families, the less competent families may believe they are, or the less they may see the need to do things themselves. Similarly, the more the focus is on what the worker does, the less opportunity there is to find out about the family's capacities.

Early on in their contact with families, workers may 'grease the wheels' by acting for the family, with their consent, on urgent matters. Getting things moving can kick-start a greater sense of optimism for the family. Providing information at the family's request can also make sense. Similarly, where communities have low reserves of social capital, workers can initiate activities that trigger social capital development. The challenge is to ensure that this behaviour does not establish a pattern of undermining people's capacity to act for themselves, necessitating the worker's involvement in more and more activity on the behalf of others and allowing less room for noticing change.

Workers can worry about expecting too much of families and reading too much into small changes. But equally there are pressures to discount change or to wait and see if something happens again before workers accept such change. Optimistic practice demands the courage to value the new as it emerges, however small a change may be.

What part do you expect your relationship with the family to play in the process of change?

> Some people might be looking to be mothered, and there may be other people in their lives who will do that for them. But it's not what I do. (Jan, family worker)

In optimistic practice the relationship that develops between the worker and the family is a starting point for change, not an end in itself. The worker is not expecting the relationship to fill a void for the family, for example, by the family seeing them as a nurturing or parenting figure who is in some way 'filling the family's tank'. The relationship workers have with families may be a very different experience from other kinds of relationships family members have had before. Within optimistic practice the focus will not be to highlight ways in which that relationship is unique, but to look at ways in which family members could incorporate more of the qualities they find positive into their relationships in general.

Trust and respect are vital to effective family work. This refers not just to the way the worker and family relate during face-to-face contact, but also to the way the worker speaks about the family outside sessions. Respect and trust are undermined where the worker speaks the language of optimism with the family but reinforces a sense of pessimism in conversations with colleagues.

Workers' reactions when they end their work with a family can also say a good deal about their expectations of the relationship. Inevitably there will be issues that may remain unresolved and challenges the family will still have to face. But just because there may be further struggles in the future does not discount what the family has achieved so far. Optimistic practice can embrace both preparing for the future, including the possibility of the family's coming back to work with the worker or agency, and celebrating the achievements of today, not just as a technique but as a genuine response to what the family has done.

How have the family's capacities been mobilised in the process of change?

> I am always concerned if people say 'I couldn't have done it without you'. I don't want families to focus on what I've done. It's what they've done that's important. (Gaye, family worker)

A key to optimistic practice is moving beyond the idea of the 'presenting problem'. What makes this shift possible is not the worker's skill in addressing the problem or in finding solutions, but the mobilisation of the family's strengths and capacities. The family may be assisted by the resources of other agencies and individuals, but these efforts are a complement rather than a substitute for what the family do themselves.

Workers can gauge their commitment to focusing on the family's capacities by listening to what happens in sessions with the family. Who does most of the talking? Does the worker spend more time listening and asking questions or explaining and advising?

It's important to recognise that it is not the worker's assessment of the family's capacities in itself that makes a difference. Optimistic practice does not rely on listing strengths or even on convincing a family or members of a community that the capacities for change are there. Change occurs through collaboration in a process in which strengths and capacities can be discovered.

A way of assessing collaboration is to ask, 'What have I learned from this family?' Workers may learn from the strategies families have developed or the things that keep them going when things are tough. Or they may learn from families' stories what it is like to have to cope with experiences they have never shared, such as being a refugee, caring for a child with a disability or surviving childhood abuse. What they learn can help them to listen more effectively and to develop a better understanding of what families find helpful.

How do you respond when things don't happen the way you'd hoped?

> I struggle with hanging on to people for too long, because I'm not comfortable with the place they've come to. When you're working with vulnerable people you have to accept that they will deal with what they want to and you may not be there to see a final resolution of the story. (Susan, adolescent worker)

Optimistic practice in no way guarantees success, however that is defined. Believing that change can happen does not ensure that it will. Seeing families angry or hurt is hard for those who have been working with them, particularly if they have seen the process of change begin but then stop. Workers' reactions at this time can say a good deal about their beliefs about families and change. Workers may feel angry and hurt too. But they don't acquire the right to blame the family for not cooperating or for being resistant to the workers' solutions. In seeking to avoid blame or judgement, workers can focus on the enormity of the family's task or their own inability to find common ground with the family. Keeping the door open to the possibility of change in the future gives change a better chance.

OPTIMISM IN CONTEXT

Family work does not occur in a vacuum. Family workers may believe that change is possible, but other influential people in the family's world may not. Families may be subject to all sorts of opinions and advice. These can have a range of impacts. Other people's ideas may be influential in the family's understanding of how a particular situation has arisen, what family members should do and what the future holds. The greater the status of the person giving their opinion in the eyes of the family, the greater impact their ideas will generally have. While the views of people with a recognised professional role can be very influential, family members and neighbours can also have a significant impact on the way the family see their situation.

> Charlie is married with a two-year-old child. He says, 'My wife was abused by her stepfather as a child. I didn't know till she got so depressed she had to go to hospital. She's on medication now, but things are still hard. I've been told that I shouldn't expect too much.'
>
> Annie is a sole parent with two children. She says, 'My grandmother raised six children of her own. She says she's never seen a child as disobedient as my Billy. She says I never should have left his dad and that what he needs is a man to keep him in line. I try not to take Billy over there now, because I go away feeling like such a useless parent.'

These influences on the family may present a challenge for workers adopting an optimistic perspective. From the family worker's point of view, the attitudes of other people in the family's life may be working to diminish the possibility of change. A range of situations may present such concerns for family workers. Sometimes the term 'medical model' is used to describe situations in which expert knowledge is given precedence over the family's knowledge of their situation. Families may experience this in a range of settings where other people take on the role of experts in their lives. The term 'medical model' is used to describe a process dominated by expert diagnosis and labelling as an end in itself, not the context in which the process occurs. There is nothing inherent in health settings to prevent staff from adopting an optimistic approach that actively respects the family's understanding of their own situation and looks beyond labels.

Sometimes family members may feel overwhelmed by the expertise of the person giving their opinion and consequently they may be unable to query it even if they are not comfortable with it or find that it does not generate helpful outcomes.

> At the clinic they told us that our daughter had a global developmental delay and that we'd be up for lots of work. That was it, then they showed us the door. Now I feel all confused. Does that mean they think she won't ever be able to look after herself or go to a normal school? Because she goes to playgroup now and fits in fine. I wish we'd never gone now, because it didn't help.

Sometimes everyone involved, including the family, may share the same understanding of how or why a problem has developed, but the family members find that the answers that others have prescribed for them are not workable. This may result in family members feeling that they are somehow at fault because they have not been able to make things work or it may contribute to them feeling that everything is hopeless.

> We all agreed that I'd have to be firmer with Josh and that he couldn't run all over me like he used to. But when I tried to stand up to him and say, 'I'm your mum, I'll say what you can do', things got worse. When I tried to put him in his room, he tore it to bits, and he screamed the house down, which meant things with the neighbours in the next flat got even worse.

Sometimes family members feel that they are being squeezed into a mould and the details of their particular experience are lost. This may occur because a particular label or diagnosis carries with it all sorts of associations that, as far as the family are concerned, don't apply to them.

> They say schizophrenia and you think of some bag lady, or someone doing something crazy in the street. It was like they couldn't possibly be talking about me.

The process of squeezing families into a mould can also happen when the worker has started from their own concerns, rather than what is happening for the particular family. If the worker's current preoccupation is with issues of grief and loss, for example, every family's experience is understood in those terms. A worker's preoccupation may reflect aspects of their personal life or external influences such as attending a particular training course.

Sometimes the family may feel caught between conflicting opinions. This can be confusing, particularly when the family's expectation is that they should be able to know the right thing to do. Family members may feel quite unequal to the task of negotiating an agreement between a range of workers and may invite the family worker, if they are perceived to be independent from the dispute, to referee.

Influential opinions may not only come from people involved in the family's life. The media and other sources of information also put forward powerful directions about how families ought to live their lives.

> They said I'd find this course helpful, because it was my first child and I was on my own. When I went I was horrified. In my home country we never put our children away from the family in a separate room to sleep. I felt really confused, because I couldn't imagine doing the things they were saying but also I wanted to do the best I could for my baby.

PROMOTING OPTIMISM

There is no formula for responding when a family are grappling with ideas that work against the belief that change is possible. The place to start is with the family's strengths, not with the resources of others. The following ideas are informed by the practice wisdom of family workers with an optimistic perspective.

1 Start from the family

To assist families, family workers need to stay focused on the family's perspective, rather than assuming that their view and the family's are the same. Sometimes workers can assume that the family share their view about what is unhelpful. In fact the family may see the situation quite differently. The family worker could inadvertently undermine the family's view if they aren't able to recognise and respect the family's experience.

> I struggle sometimes when children are diagnosed as having Attention Deficit Disorder, or ADD. Sometimes I'm aware that the same children have been exposed to domestic violence, and the ADD label can mean that their trauma is overlooked when it may

be a precipitating factor to the behaviour that has led to the diagnosis. But I have to go with what the family know at the time, rather than trying to force my view on them. For parents there can be an enormous sense of relief that their difficulties with their children are related to an external diagnosis when they themselves have felt labelled as 'bad parents'. That helps them because they feel more in control. That can then create an opportunity for us to work with them on strategies that are helpful for the child. (Glenys, service coordinator)

2 Explore how ideas fit for the family

A diagnosis can sometimes make people feel that they have been boxed in and that the label will now determine the course of their life. An alternative approach is to focus on ways in which that knowledge contained in a diagnosis does or does not fit for the family. This can open up the possibility of family members taking what is useful for them without feeling as if they are being stereotyped.

A diagnosis can also help the family to make contact through self-help groups with others who have had similar experiences. The family may also choose to see the label as a sort of shorthand or a cover story, a quick way to access something that is helpful. That does not mean they have to wear the label 24 hours a day. The family need to feel in control of the label, not as if the label is controlling them.

> Cheryl is working with a family where Brian, aged six, has been diagnosed with a neurological disorder. There was a bit of dispute among the doctors about the diagnosis and the message the family were given was that in a few years the diagnosis would be more conclusive. The family initially felt resentful that they weren't given a definitive answer for Brian's difficulties. They found it difficult to understand how different specialists could disagree. Cheryl obtained more information about the diagnosed condition and the family joined a support group where they met other parents. They found contact with other parents helpful and they decided that they'd use the diagnosis where it seemed useful, for example, so that teachers at Brian's school would realise he had special needs. However, as Brian's dad put it, they wouldn't treat it as a life sentence.

If family members decide that the knowledge being offered to them does not fit, the possibility of looking for other information that fits better for them opens up. This helps people move away from a search for labels and focuses attention on the usefulness of particular services and interventions.

> Lillian had been diagnosed as having schizophrenia. She was very uncomfortable with that label because of the implications for her children, as schizophrenia can be considered to have a genetic component. She'd had many difficult experiences in her life, and she felt much more comfortable with the idea that she had post-traumatic stress disorder. It enabled her to acknowledge that she needed to be mindful of issues about her mental health and to use medication to manage some of those, without her having to take on some of the schizophrenia label's associations.

3 Generate an alternative view

Sometimes when a family worker has doubts about the helpfulness of particular ideas or explanations it may be helpful to simply disregard them. This frees the worker to focus on the ideas that seem to fit best with the family at the time, without being involved in disputes about which opinion is right.

> Cherry approached a family service because she was at her wit's end about what to do with nine-year-old Emma. They'd seen specialists and had lots of investigations. They'd tried medication without much success. Cherry said that Emma had been diagnosed with ADD, but another specialist had said she had oppositional disorder. Cherry's mother believed that Emma should be exorcised for demon possession. Cherry had withstood her mother's pressure to take that course of action, but had been deeply shaken by the suggestion and hadn't dismissed it completely. The family worker spent time hearing Cherry and Emma's story and responding to the confusion and hurt they both felt, but stayed right out of the question about what was the 'real' problem. They talked instead about what the family was up against and discovered some habits that had taken root in the family while their attention had been elsewhere. After the first conversations during which Cherry and Emma talked about all the different explanations people had offered, there was no more discussion about any of the labels. As the family sorted out the habits, Cherry and Emma just didn't seem to feel that the labels and explanations were as important any more.

4 Acknowledge the family's expertise

In the face of expert advice, it is easy for family members to doubt their competence and to feel that if the expert's advice doesn't work for them, they are at fault. Sometimes providing opportunities for people to remind themselves about what they know, and giving them permission to examine the expert's advice in the light of that knowledge, can help them feel more confident and to put advice into a more useful context.

> There are lots of parenting programs around that tell people how they should manage their children. Aspects of those programs can be very useful, but sometimes people feel overwhelmed by them, and if they can't put all the ideas into practice straight away they feel like they've failed. When we run groups for parents we sometimes take some of this material and encourage them to question it. This can be a bit of a shock for people who assume that if it's in a book or on a video then it must be right. But when they get beyond that they can start saying things like 'I wouldn't actually do it that way' and identifying what they think works for them. Of course quite a bit of parenting material is presented by men when it is generally women who do most of the work. Pointing this out in itself can generate some interesting discussions. It can also be fun and it helps parents to feel comfortable with finding out what works for them and their children, rather than being enslaved by expert advice. (Di, family worker)

PRACTISING OPTIMISM

> I don't find it hard to be optimistic when things are going well with a family with whom I'm working. Sometimes signs of change are just jumping out all over the place. It's much harder to practise optimism when everything's falling apart, and each phone call or knock on the door brings a new message of disaster. Sometimes just finding a small thing to like or admire in a person can make such a difference. Something like the fact that they always offer you a cup of coffee or the thriving pot plants by their door.
>   As a worker, you can get overwhelmed by your own doubts, especially when other people around the family have given up. You have to keep reminding yourself that an optimistic perspective is not just a way of explaining why things are working. It's a choice

workers must make about the stance they take in their work. Practising optimism means remembering to behave as if change is possible. Working with the family as if change is impossible is a waste of time. (Bronwyn, family worker)

nine

Optimism on another level: working with other agencies

Amanda manages a family service in a large city. She says, 'Sure, the work is demanding, and there are never enough resources to go around. When you see families going down you always ask what more you could have done even when you feel like you've done all you could. Then we also see families making major changes in their lives, which is incredibly exciting. But often it feels like the hardest part of our work is dealing with other agencies. People can be so precious about their work, it's like they are the centre of the universe. They get defensive, and sometimes it's like they lose sight of what they are actually there to do.'

Amanda's experiences of the demands of working with other agencies are shared by many family workers. Family service agencies provide practical assistance, counselling and group work, emergency accommodation and respite care for children, to name just a few vital programs. But the range of organisations that can have an impact on the lives of families is much broader than agencies with a specifically family focus. Education, health care, employment services, housing, transport and local government are just some of the other agencies that shape the options available for families.

Workers in family services can lose sight of the fact that they are only part of the picture. Families may only be involved with a service for a few months. They will need housing, transport and health care for the rest of their lives. Unless workers look at the bigger picture they can miss out on opportunities to access resources that could assist families and have less ability to influence decisions that can transform families' lives. Working with local residents and other agencies to install some decent playground equipment and a basketball court in the local park may be a very strategic way to improve the situation for local children.

To maximise possibilities for change for families, a wide range of agencies need to be able to work together. If agencies want to encourage positive, cooperative relationships within families, it makes sense that organisations also need to practise cooperation in the way they work together. Why is it, then, that cooperative relationships between organisations can be so hard to achieve?

While families may benefit from agencies being able to work together in a coordinated way, cooperation does not necessarily maximise the individual interests of the agency. In all sorts of ways agencies are under pressure to compete. This includes competition for funding and demarcation disputes to establish which particular agency should deliver services.

Jenny, an experienced family worker, expresses her frustrations at the blocks to building partnerships with other agencies. As she explains, 'Now agencies are required to tender for funding it forces people to be competitive. You have winners and losers when it comes to money. The effect that has on agency relationships doesn't go away once the money has been allocated. It means everyone is very conscious about the image of their agency, and no one wants to be seen to make mistakes. That gets in the way of people learning from each other's experience, and it means when agency workers disagree, it makes it harder for anyone to back down.

'When new programs are set up everyone wants a piece of the action. They all make the most of their expertise, and put down what anyone else is doing. It's amazing how the end result seems to be that everyone feels insecure and defensive. If you talk to people employed by government departments or people in non-government agencies, they are all worried that someone on the other side of the fence is out to get them. If families felt this strongly we'd be talking about paranoia!'

Some of the challenges intrinsic to family work have a powerful impact on relationships between agencies. Working with people who feel powerless can affect the way family workers see their own situation.

> Leslie and Jim were referred to a family service because they had financial difficulties and they were having difficulties in their relationships. They were really struggling with the care of Eddie, who had multiple disabilities and very challenging behaviour. The family wanted respite care once a month and they needed it right away. The respite care service could not find a family able to cope with Eddie's particular needs straight away and Leslie and Jim became very angry. In some ways it was easier for them to be angry with the respite care service than to talk about some of the other things they were facing. The family worker, Mattie, started to feel angry with the respite care service. Mattie explains: 'One of my colleagues made me think about what I was saying about the respite service. It was understandable that Leslie and Jim felt angry. But the respite care staff were doing the best they could with the resources they had. It didn't help anyone, particularly Leslie, Jim and Eddie, if I got angry too. Blaming the respite care service for the situation made no more sense than blaming Leslie and Jim.'

Working with people who are vulnerable and in situations where there are real concerns about safety can shape the way workers do their job and the pressures they feel when working with staff outside their own agency. Sometimes the feelings of the staff become the focus of attention, rather than the needs of the families.

Change is not just an issue for families individually or in communities. Family workers can also become stuck in entrenched positions in their relationships with other agencies, both those that specialise in families and those with wider responsibilities, and can end up feeling that they have nowhere to go. The optimistic stance developed in this book applies just as much to these situations as it does to families. This chapter examines ways in which workers have used optimistic approaches to address challenges in their work with other agencies and identifies some of the strategies that are shared by different approaches to optimistic practice in interagency work.

The discoveries described here are not necessarily new or unique to a particular approach. Family workers could use various approaches and come up with similar discoveries. The approaches are a reference point for workers feeling stuck in their relationships with other agencies and looking for possibilities for change.

USING THE SOLUTION-FOCUSED APPROACH:
BECOMING A SOLUTION BUILDER

Solution-focused work emphasises finding what works in a situation and extending that. This approach helps workers minimise the time they spend focusing on problems and shifts attention to what works. Workers can spend a good deal of time and emotion dwelling on problems with other agencies. Rather than assisting them to generate solutions, these conversations can often contribute to them feeling more stuck and hopeless. The 'miracle question' that workers often find helpful with families can apply to work with other agencies as well. 'Suppose there was a miracle, and the difficulties between agencies disappeared. How would you notice? What would be different?'

Jules, a family worker, talks about her experience in the family support service in which she works. 'We were sitting in a team meeting one day and we were bagging the social workers at the hospital. They never referred to our groups and only used us if they thought we could do something very concrete for a family. Someone said, almost as a joke, "I think we're stuck in a whole lot of problem talk here." It shook us up a bit, because we realised that it was problem talk, and we'd never talk that way about a family. We decided to consciously apply the same ideas we'd use with families to the situation with the hospital. We thought about whether there had been a time when we'd had the kind of contact with them that had worked well. We recognised there had been two times over the last year that had been different. They had both involved staff who'd come more recently, but we hadn't recognised that as significant at the time. We then thought about what we did with agencies with whom we had good relationships and recognised we did give much less feedback to the hospital team, and we also didn't bother to send them information about groups we were running and so on.

'Over the next few months we made sure we included them in any mailouts, and we made more of an effort when we had contact either through referrals or at interagency level. I think we've got more in common with some of the staff there than others, but there has been a definite shift in the way we work with many of them. This has benefited families. Last week one of them rang us to refer a family to one of our parenting groups. That wouldn't have happened before.'

USING THE NARRATIVE APPROACH: OPENING SPACE FOR A PREFERRED STORY

In narrative work, externalising helps workers to move away from a polarised view where the good agency is pitted against the bad agency. Externalising can also be useful where people see the difficulty in terms of the personality of someone from another agency. Accounts of difficulties that centre on personality can powerfully contribute to feelings of hopelessness and frustration, because it is generally understood that someone's personality will be unlikely to change.

Often all parties are feeling oppressed and pushed around by the difficulties in their relationships. If they can see the problem as 'out there', it can be possible to build on their common experience and develop a preferred story that opens possibilities for cooperation.

Staff at Meadowvale Family Centre were feeling very negative about the local school. Several families they had been working with had had children suspended from school, which put enormous pressure on those families. Lee, one of the workers at the centre, explained: 'We had got to the point where we just raised our eyebrows in disgust every time the school was mentioned. We described it as cold and heartless. As chance had it, two of us attended a child protection meeting that the school principal attended as well. We got into conversation and were a bit stunned at what we heard.

'The school had been under enormous pressure from staffing problems, and the principal acknowledged quite frankly that the instability had been very unsettling for some children and had contributed to the suspensions. Many of the school staff had been very distressed about these events, but had felt helpless. As we talked we had a sense that we'd all been affected by the climate of uncertainty. It just made all the difference to how we saw the situation. Back at the office we sent the principal some pamphlets about our service so she knew what we could offer families. A month later the principal asked our staff to morning tea to judge the Easter hat parade. It was a little thing, but going there and meeting the staff got things moving. Last term we ran a parenting course at the school for the parents, and had a great response from the teachers as well.'

Developing an alternative story does not require all parties to be actively committed to this process. However, it does require that some of the participants move beyond blaming and work from the position that the other agency is not the problem.

USING A COGNITIVE APPROACH: CHANGING WAYS OF THINKING

The cognitive approach provides a process for identifying and challenging irrational or unhelpful thoughts. Interagency issues shared among team members provide fertile ground for amplifying irrational or unhelpful ideas. Resource inequities and rivalries between professional groups can also fuel the development of such ideas. It is not unusual for workers to feel that someone from another agency wants to intimidate them or harm their career, or to feel that a family are being deliberately victimised by staff from another service. There may be occasional times when such thoughts are well-founded. But when they are not, these beliefs can be very damaging to interagency relationships with negative consequences for families.

A family centre was working with Trudi and her children who were in a very complicated situation. The school was involved and the housing department, the police, the court support service and another counselling service also had a role. Workers from the family centre said, 'We recognised how hard Trudi had worked, and we were frustrated with how little support some of the other agencies involved were prepared to offer. At the same time there were times when Trudi kept everyone in the dark about what was really happening at home, particularly in relation to her partner.

'We were getting pretty uptight about it all, and we started to believe that Trudi was being set up by another agency. We thought that they were not interested in helping Trudi and her family, just in collecting negative information to feed to the statutory child protection department. We really didn't want to deal with them. Because that agency is quite a big one, we felt very pessimistic that we could do anything about that. When a case conference was called, we thought there was no point in going.

'We have a supervisor who comes in once a month to meet with us. When we started to describe the situation, the supervisor focused on some of the beliefs underlying these thoughts. She helped us identify some more helpful ways of thinking. For instance, rather than saying that there's nothing we can do, we focused on the information we could offer about Trudi's family. It was an interesting experience to use with ourselves some of the ideas we use with families, and it certainly made a difference, for us and for Trudi.'

USING A COMMUNITY-BUILDING APPROACH: CREATING SOCIAL FABRIC

Community building involves activities that promote trust, bring diverse groups together and develop networks. While networking has long been recognised as a key strategy in interagency relationships, thinking about social capital helps to identify ways in which networking can be most effective.

Communities with low reserves of social capital often have low levels of trust and limited networks between community agencies. This places families in double jeopardy and highlights the importance of agencies giving priority to activities that can develop social capital as a resource for change.

Tirrania is with an agency that specialises in work with families affected by drugs or alcohol in a low-income area. She says, 'As a small service we are very isolated structurally and it is particularly important that we have links. I really think that to work well with other organisations, it is important to develop trust and to be able to handle different approaches to tackling issues.

'We've put some time into developing relationships that take us a bit outside our usual contacts. For example, I met the president of the Chamber of Commerce at a local function, and contacted him afterwards and met him to have a coffee. Through him I met the council's director of community services. He was able to help us access venues for meetings, and invited me onto the council's safety committee. That put me in touch with some other key people. You don't necessarily know what the benefits of those links will be when you start the process.

'The small size of our organisation allows us to be flexible and innovative in a way that's harder for large organisations. However, it is easy to become stuck in a victim position and feel like we are not that important because we are small. The concept of social capital empowers us and helps us to hold onto the importance of mutual respect, irrespective of size and resources. It is useful in rethinking dynamics and power relationships between organisations. We have approached people at the top of government departments and other organisations, believing it is possible to have a mutual, trusting working relationship. We have found these people have been prepared to give their time and other resources to develop new ways of working together. The organisation is becoming stronger and I am sure that the use of the community-building approach is a major key to this. We're not just seeing families, we're working to change the system.'

OPTIMISM IN INTERAGENCY RELATIONSHIPS

Just as in work with families individually and in communities, putting optimism into practice in interagency relationships involves believing change can happen and looking to the capacities of the agencies and their staff, rather than locating the responsibility for change outside the agencies involved. Some common themes emerge from review of the strategies generated from optimistic thinking about interagency work.

1 Finding common ground

As the preceding stories illustrate, finding common ground can be the key to challenging past unhelpful patterns in relationships with other agencies. Common ground can mean a shared concern or goal or it may mean simply being together in the same physical space. Focusing on what workers have in common, rather than on their differences, goes a long way towards changing their beliefs and expectations.

> We were having lots of difficulty with our relationship with the local child protection authority. When we rang them up with a report, we'd get confusing messages and it felt like nothing would happen. We ended up ringing up some of the staff, and going out for a coffee. We found out more about the constraints they were working under and they felt more able to trust us. We found it easier then to ring them up, and talk in a more respectful and less defensive way. We were able to ring up and consult them, rather than making a formal report straight away. (Greg, family counsellor)

2 Taking a risk

Just as families struggle with their early attempts to make change happen, workers will not necessarily find working for better relationships with other agencies a comfortable experience, especially at first. Someone has to make the first move or nothing will change. Sometimes those first moves will go nowhere, but other times the results can be a surprise.

We'd had real difficulties with the child protection agency and felt that we were being undermined. I was lucky we have a close team and I had their support. We spent time talking about the situation. We decided that the difficulties in our relationship with this agency weren't helping the families we worked with, and we needed to do something. We began by trying to create one-to-one relationships with staff members. There were some we couldn't establish contact with, but we worked with the ones where we could. We started to understand that they were under-resourced as well. We also developed a better understanding of their role. Two years later, things are very different. When we invited them to a barbecue not long ago, most of them came. It's been good for the families we work with too, because they now understand that the agency staff don't want to take their kids. (Jan, service coordinator)

3 Watching out for strategic moments

Change may always be possible, but it is more likely to come at some times rather than others. Watching for openings for change can help make workers make the most of their efforts. Often the most strategic moments are when something has changed somewhere already. The arrival of a new staff member in an organisation, a new policy proposal, a change in government legislation, even moving offices—all these can be strategic points to address agency relationships. All are times when it may be easier to bring people together with some kind of common purpose, even if it is just a cup of tea in the new office. Sometimes when change seems unlikely it can be helpful just to look for a change somewhere and think about how to make something of it.

When we started using a shared approach to our work it did create a bit of confusion. It was hard for the child protection authority, because it fundamentally changed the way we worked. They were worried about where the ideas had come from because it wasn't the way they were used to working. We organised a workshop for the agencies we worked with, so that we could explain the principles and how we were putting them into practice. It meant we could be clear about what was different and they could be reassured that we did know what we were doing. Over time other agencies in town have adopted the same approach, which helps us to work together. (Robyn, service coordinator)

4 Starting small

From working with families it is evident that first steps do not have to be big to have an effect. It also doesn't matter so much if they don't seem to have much impact. The exciting part of starting with something small is watching for the ripples after the initial impact.

> When this centre was first envisioned, we knew we wanted to work in partnership with other agencies, but we didn't know what that would mean. We started with a very ordinary building and a desire to build connections. Building partnerships comes down to building relationships. We had a key contact with the local nursing unit manager, and that enabled us to bring not only early childhood nurses but also community midwives into the centre. That gives us tremendous access to families even before children are born. Now we run all sorts of groups, we have a home visiting service, and we are training and using volunteers. They were small steps in the beginning, but now we're on the run. (Kate, centre coordinator)

THE ACTIVE PRACTICE OF OPTIMISM

Practising optimism is an ongoing challenge for family workers. The grounds for pessimism can often seem overwhelming. It is so much easier to stereotype or dismiss family members and their experiences than it is to genuinely share and understand what it means to live with their day-to-day situation. At the same time, retaining a focus on families' capacities must constantly be balanced with a perception of family members' current realities, particularly in relation to children. An openness to optimism may also increase family workers' vulnerability to disappointment and a sense of failure in their work.

For workers with a large case load, limited resources and often inadequate support, it can be hard to allow space for optimism. Yet many family workers, including those whose experiences are described in this book, have found ways to make room for optimism in their practice.

While some people naturally have a more positive disposition than others, practising optimism as described in this book is not primarily a matter of personality. Optimistic practice is a sign of the operation of core values in family work. Central to these are the belief that change is possible and the focus on the family members' capacities as the starting point for change.

If workers believe that change is possible and that it starts with people's strengths and capacities, the way they work will have a similar flavour, whether it is with individual families, communities or other agencies. Optimism is not primarily a practice tool or a strategic intervention. Its relevance to family work is a reflection of its significance on a larger scale.

In an interview, the Australian novelist Tim Winton shared some thoughts on the topic of practising optimism:

> I myself am not naturally optimistic. I suffer dark moods and sometimes I see more obstacles than I really need to see, so I've found that optimism as a discipline has been quite useful . . .
>
> When something is there to be seen that is positive it has to be acknowledged because those things are just too easy to let slip through your fingers. There's too much darkness to overwhelm you. I think it's just a matter of giving those things due account when they come along. (Winton 1998)

References

Bachelor, Alexander, and Horvath, Adam (1999) 'The Therapeutic Relationship' in Hubble, Mark, Duncan, Barry, and Miller, Scott (eds) *The Heart and Soul of Change: What Works in Therapy*, American Psychological Association, Washington

Beck, Aaron, Wright, Fred, Newman, Cory, and Liese, Bruce (1993) *Cognitive Therapy of Substance Abuse*, Guilford Press, New York

Beck, Judith (1995) *Cognitive Therapy: Basics and Beyond*, Guilford Press, New York

Bullen, Paul (1998) *Strengthening Families: Family Support Services in NSW*, Family Support Services Association of NSW, Sydney

Bullen, Paul, with Onyx, Jenny (1999) *Social Capital: Family Support Services and Neighbourhood and Community Centres in NSW*, Management Alternatives, Sydney

Cox, Eva (1995) *A Truly Civil Society*, ABC Books, Sydney

Family Support Services in NSW (1998) *1998 Statewide Data Collection*, Family Support Services Association of NSW, Sydney

Farmer, Elaine, and Owen, Morag (1995) *Child Protection Practice: Private Risks and Public Remedies, Decision-making, Interventions and Outcomes in Child Protection*, HMSO, London

Freedman, Jill, and Combs, Gene (1996) *Narrative Therapy: The Social Construction of Preferred Realities*, W.W. Norton, New York

Garbarino, James, and Kostelny, Kathleen (1994) 'Family Support and Community Development' in Kagan, Sharon, and Weissbourd,

Bernice (eds) *Putting Families First: America's Family Support Movement and the Challenge of Change*, Jossey-Bass, San Francisco

Putnam, Robert (1993) 'The Prosperous Community: Social Capital and Public Life', *American Prospect*, 13: 35–42

Reder, Peter, Duncan, Sylvia, and Gray, Moria (1993) *Beyond Blame*, Routledge, London

Scott, Dorothy, and O'Neil, Di (1998) *Beyond Child Rescue*, Solution Press, Victoria

Seligman, Martin, Reivich, Karen, Jaycox, Lisa, and Gilham, Jane (1995) *The Optimistic Child*, Random House, Sydney

Snyder, C.R., Michael, Scott, and Cheavens, Jennifer (1999) 'Hope as a Psychotherapeutic Foundation of Common Factors, Placebos and Experiences' in Hubble, Mark, Duncan, Barry, and Miller, Scott, *The Heart and Soul of Change: What Works in Therapy*, American Psychological Association, Washington

Vinson, Tony, Baldry, Eileen, and Hargreaves, Jane (1996) 'Neighbourhood, Networks and Child Abuse', *British Journal of Social Work*, 26: 523–43

Webster-Stratton, Carolyn (1997) 'From Parent Training to Community Building', *Families in Society*, 78: 156–71

White, Michael (1997) *Narratives of Therapists' Lives*, Dulwich Centre Publications, Adelaide

White, Michael, and Epston, David (1990) *Narrative Means to Therapeutic Ends*, W.W. Norton, New York

Winton, Tim (1998) 'Radio National Arts Today', Tim Winton in conversation with Julie Rigg, ABC Radio National, 7 September

Index